SURVIVOR'S GUIDE

for

MEN IN DIVORCE

*A Candid Manual for Men
on Family Law 'Street Smarts'*

JOHNNY PETERSON JD

Retired Family Law Attorney

DISCLAIMER: This book is written strictly for educational purposes. It cannot replace legal advice from an experienced family law attorney who is fully aware of all the facts of your case. It is strongly recommended that anyone facing family law issues seek legal advice from an experienced family law attorney who practices law in your area. Purchasing or reading this book does not create an attorney-client relationship, nor are any statements herein legal advice..

TABLE OF CONTENTS
PART I

PART II

PART I

CHAPTER 1

THE FAMILY LAW ENVIRONMENT

In order to understand family law, a person needs to grasp the critical concepts of the laws that carry the day in court. Besides understanding the fundamental principles of the law, it is crucial that men facing divorce understand how to use that knowledge to their advantage within the family law environment.

All too often, people, including attorneys, and even judges listening to unenlightened attorneys, can't see the forest for the trees. In the later Nutshell Chapters, you will learn the critical aspects of the law as they relate to the facts of your case. Besides understanding your legal position on your family law issues, use this book to understand how your strategies, decisions, actions, and even demeanor can dramatically influence the outcome of your family law issues when you're playing your cards and positioning yourself in the family law environment.

When I refer to the "family law environment," I am not simply referring to the time spent in the courtroom in front of the judge. I am referring to *anything and everything* dealing with and relating to the resolution of your family law issues. This includes how you relate to your opponent and to her attorney. It includes how you relate to your own attorney, to the judge, and to anyone else who may have an impact on the resolution of your case.

To truly master family law you should understand "family law street smarts." In other words, you should have a practical, common sense understanding of how family law issues are dealt with and adjudicated within our family court system. This includes knowing the dos and don'ts along with adopting common sense strategies that improve a person's odds of obtaining a favorable result.

Legally, you are the boss on how to proceed with your court matters. *It's you, not your attorney, which must make the key decisions on how to proceed with your case!* Attorneys have the legal and ethical duty to inform their clients of this important fact at the beginning of their attorney-client relationships.

It's your signature on any negotiated settlement. It's your decision if you want to litigate any or all of your family law issues. Your attorney is your legal counselor, paper pusher, negotiator, and voice. Your attorney works for you. It's your job to make it easier for your attorney to advocate for you. Not only will it help reduce your attorney's billable fees, it will contribute to the overall quality of your representation.

The laws in this country are a convoluted mass of changing rules, regulations, and penalties passed down by many over countless years. The foundation of all our laws was passed down to us directly from England during our early colonial period when we were a part of the British Empire. By their very nature, laws change over time and are continuing to do so today.

Laws change because political and social attitudes within societies change. It often takes time for laws to change to reflect the changing times and social attitudes. Due to the manner in which laws are created and modified within our legislative system, laws are often written poorly and ripe for different interpretations. Inequality, whether in the law itself or in the enforcement of the law, has historically been a problem within American jurisprudence, and frankly still is.

Our highest legal scholars in their medieval black robes sitting on the bench in our appellate and supreme courts across the land have been given the power to interpret the law as it should be applied to individual cases. Yet they often scratch their heads in bewilderment while handing down split decisions from mundane matters all the way to whether the states have the power to execute people for their crimes.

Laws that appear well written often take on different meanings years later due to changing social attitudes and predispositions. Take for instance the changing meanings of the Equal Protection Clause of the Fourteenth Amendment to the United States Constitution. Written just after the Civil War, our society has struggled with the meaning of the Equal Protection Clause even though the meaning appears crystal clear. The Equal Protection Clause states that "no State shall... deny to any person within its jurisdiction the equal protection of the laws."

Societies have been creating and enforcing laws since prehistoric times to establish social control, morality, and individual justice according to what they believe is just and appropriate. Regardless of the original intent justifying the enactment of any particular law, be aware that laws can lead to grave injustices.

I can't help but think of the injustices that occurred in our *relatively* recent American past when our lawmakers with our judges' nods of approval enforced slavery, engaged in countless atrocities against Native Americans for their land, and even actively embraced gender discrimination against women.

The Equal Protection Clause of the Fourteenth Amendment is a good law, but its enforcement to protect against unequal enforcement of the law is still being challenged by those who prefer that things remain unequal.

With hindsight, we can say those despicable acts against our fellow human beings were unjust. Looking back with 20-20 vision, it is easy to realize that the majority of people within our society were simply going with the flow while rationalizing that their actions were in accordance with the status quo.

People often act on self-righteousness, egotism, and majority benefit over a weaker minority while maintaining, and *even believing* that they were acting justly even when they were clearly not, at least not according to our current sense of justice and morality.

3

This irresolvable irony can be explained by defining *justice*. Justice is a fluid concept that a society defines based on its social beliefs, values, and norms, which inevitably change over time. Many famous philosophers have defined justice more to my liking, suggesting some sort of divine spiritual influence that determines right from wrong, and justice from injustice. But most fail to incorporate how changing social belief systems affect humans' sense of morality and justice, and what is right from what is wrong.

Family law is the term used to define the laws and regulations relating to marriages and divorces. *As a general rule*, individual state laws are quite similar from state to state. True, there are some notable exceptions and different enforcements of individual state laws, but these differences are often overemphasized. The overemphasis on the subtle differences among individual state laws can make a person lose sight of the critical concepts within the law that usually carry the day in courts across the country.

Laws are enforced in three different types of court proceedings. The three main types of court proceedings are called *criminal court proceedings*, *civil court proceedings*, and *administrative court proceedings*.

Divorces and other family law matters, like paternity suits and child support actions, are tried in *civil court proceedings*. The procedural rules used during divorce hearings and other family law hearings are quite different from those used during criminal court proceedings. Criminal court proceedings offer greater procedural safeguards for criminal defendants than the procedural safeguards that are used to protect family law litigants from unfair court rulings.

There are many different types of civil court proceedings. For instance, negligence cases for personal injury are civil court proceedings. Similarly, breach of contract cases are also handled in civil court. Even though family law cases are civil court actions, *there are far fewer procedural safeguards in family court than in regular civil court proceedings.*

For one thing, juries are not allowed in family court. This gives judges the power to interpret the facts of a case as they see fit. Another thing is that judges are given far more discretionary powers on family law matters than other areas of the law.

In family court, only one person determines the truthfulness of the facts presented to the court and then has the absolute power to determine what is fair and just to resolve family court cases. That person is the judge.

Court jurisdiction refers to the *power* that a court has to hear and resolve a case. Court jurisdiction thus determines the location of a courtroom where a case is to be tried. Generally speaking, *the laws applied to a family law case are the laws of the state where the courtroom is actually located.* If personal real estate is located in a different state, the division of that real estate might be according to law where the real estate is located (if different). By contrast, the law of the state or country where a couple was married is only relevant in determining whether a couple was actually legally married or not.

Usually, the most important jurisdictional factor to determine *where* a divorce is to be tried is only a matter of determining where the parties are residing when one of the parties decides to Petition for Dissolution of the Marriage. There are various exceptions to this general rule. These exceptions usually involve residency issues within a different county or state, or even within a different country.

It is no secret that judges decisions are often affected by their mood on a particular day. It is well known that the facts relevant to a particular case are often interpreted and weighed differently by different judges. Like everyone else, judges have their own individual belief systems complete with their own personal biases and points of view. And like anyone else, judges can jump to conclusions. In our overworked court system, a judge might even size up a case due to initial impressions of the litigants by the way they look and act the very first day in the courtroom.

Avoid negative nonverbal communications through body language when you are dealing in the family court environment. Have you ever heard the expression "first impressions are often lasting impressions"? How you look and act along with your general demeanor does make a difference on how you will be judged, not only by the judge, but also by the other important players involved in your case, all the way down to your own attorney.

Beware: an unfair ruling in a family civil court case can sting worse than a guilty conviction for a serious crime in criminal court. There are *very* credible arguments that the enforcement of family law as it exists today, including the actual written state laws themselves, seriously violate this country's fundamental civil rights laws. These violations include the Abolition of Involuntary Servitude (slavery), Due Process (the right to a fair hearing by a neutral third party), Equal Protection of the Law, the right not to be subject to Unreasonable Searches and Seizures, Sexual Discrimination, the Right to Privacy, and the Abolition of Debtor's Prison.

It is extremely important to realize that judges are given vast discretionary powers when deciding family law cases. Their discretionary power includes their power to determine what is fair and "equitable" under a particular set of circumstances. A judge's discretionary power in family court vastly exceeds discretionary power in criminal court proceedings, and even exceeds their discretionary power in other types of civil court proceedings.

Frankly, there is very little control over a judge's power in family court even when a judge makes an unfair decision. True, a court of appeals can overturn a judge's decision, but only when it is found in the record that the judge's decision was manifestly unjust, clearly erroneous, or a clear abuse of discretion. Appellate courts give great deference to the decisions judges make in the lower courts, and their standards of review weed out all but the most egregious conduct.

I hate to be the bearer of bad news, but the law shifted years ago. In the past women were discriminated against in everyday life; now *men— yes, men*—are still commonly discriminated against in family court. This is due in part to the simple economics involving billions of dollars annually, greed, and reverse discrimination. It is also largely due to the very nature of our overworked family court system.

I don't deny that the application of American law is fairer than that of many other countries, where a man might get his arm cut off for stealing a loaf of bread to support his family. But there are very serious injustices occurring regularly in our family court system. Family law courts have not kept up with the changing status of women, from a period of time not that long ago when women desperately needed preferential treatment in family court in order to help them even their odds in a male-dominated society. I beg to differ with those who believe we are still in a male-dominated society to the extent that women require preferential treatment from the courts to help even the odds.

When you are confronted with an eight-hundred-pound, black-robed gorilla looking down on you from the court bench (your judge), you should minimize your odds for a bad outcome by understanding the common pitfalls that happen every day to other average Joes who find themselves getting screwed in family court. Why not learn from their failures and success stories in order to acquire your own effective strategies to maximize your odds? When figuring out what type of strategy to take, you should factor in common sense dos and don'ts which are applicable to the family court environment.

When you have an informed strategy, it will help you advocate your case. Equally important, it will help you negotiate your position intelligently and civilly with the opposing side. A fair Negotiated Settlement always trumps needless litigation that could have been avoided.

You can ill afford to make a "pointless point" out of spite and anger. An overly aggressive approach weakens your credibility on the issues you should be focusing on, and it can make you look like the bad guy even if you're not. If your approach is too passive, there's a good possibility you could get railroaded. If you start making serious strategic blunders in the family court environment from the get-go due to your ignorance of the law and the family court environment, your fate could be sealed—just another average Joe who got screwed in family court. You definitely want to avoid that slippery slope. To help even the odds in family court, you should acquire a sense of family law street smarts to guide you through the mine fields.

From the very onset of your divorce, your goal should be to come up with a fair resolution of your case with your opponent. This strategy can help avoid getting into an ugly scorched-earth campaign during a divorce. If you allow things to get truly nasty during a divorce, be fully aware that men usually get scorched far worse than women do simply because our society has historically given women preferential treatment in family court. When you are going through a divorce, having a good strategy is your sword and knowing the common pitfalls that men face in our family court environment is your shield.

A divorce can easily turn into a living hell that can drive a person crazy. Listen to the advice of your family and friends and take care of yourself emotionally. Obsessing and allowing your spirit and zest for life to be damaged only hurts you, your family, and friends. What's worse is that your pain can easily turn out to be your opponent's gain in the family court environment because it can lead to stupid mistakes. You need a cool head and detached rational thinking during this time of emotional upheaval. Hopefully by reading this book you will develop key insights that you will need to help resolve your current situation.

Your former loving wife can easily turn out to be your worst enemy. *Do you think that there is any average Joe* out there who married his so-called soul mate with the expectation that his legally married wife would later turn on him and take him to family court with the sole intent to take him to the cleaners with a scorched-earth policy? Don't think to yourself, "Nah, she would never do something like that to me. I know her too well. She'd never trash all of our good memories and life experiences we've had." *Expect the unexpected.* Be a survivor and don't allow yourself to be easily victimized. Don't ignore the red flags that may be popping up like poppies in a poppy field.

Know that women are very much aware they have an advantage in family court. *It's just that plain and simple.* The disadvantage that men face in family court is compounded when their adversaries become aggressive and willing to use every trick in the book for their means to an end, whether ethical or not. Whether you realize it or not, you have an adversary. *The first of several key strategies you should adopt is to think defensively.*

Don't underestimate your potential challenges or how adversarial, or even immoral, your opponent may turn out to be. Don't be sideswiped or sucker punched because of disbelief in this important statement. If you believe that our court system is overwhelmingly fair and just regarding the application of family law in America as it exists today, you need not read any further. *This book is written to help even the odds for the average Joe facing divorce.*

CHAPTER 2

IMMEDIATE ADVICE

If your marriage is going to hell or has already gone to hell, be careful how you act. Don't go throw gas on the fire and think it might somehow help matters. I assure you that you'll be getting yourself into dangerous territory that could come back to haunt you if you proceed recklessly with your mouth.

Heated, belittling arguments never sway any hearts or minds. A man who thinks he can win an argument with an angry headstrong woman just isn't thinking clearly. The only thing that might be gained from that kind of ridiculous approach is to increase the possibility of creating an adversary from hell in divorce court.

Don't kid yourself: your wife, or soon-to-be ex-wife, whichever it may be, is fully aware that she has a distinct advantage over you in the family court environment simply because of her gender. If she rattles her swords, don't rattle yours. It's a red flag that trouble is brewing. Observe rather than allowing your primal instincts to lead you to react in kind.

Family court is nothing like television court dramas where the flashiest suits and the most dramatic courtroom rhetoric prevail. It is *more* like a bad dream where you can find yourself in slow motion continuously unable to run away fast enough from a *known* impending danger. That result is all too likely to occur in family court when a man plays what cards he has wrong, especially if the divorcing wife is acting unethically.

As a litigant in a lawsuit, your actions and inactions can either help or hurt the possibility of your obtaining a fair result in family court. Take time to think things over. *Consider the likely consequences* of different alternative courses of action. It will help you to choose the most logical ways to proceed.

Not surprisingly, when the crap hits the fan, many people become stunned and too unfocused to *logically* try to think things out. This can happen when a person endures the constant stress of having to deal with the adversarial and confrontational matters that arise in the family law environment. As a default method, many choose to follow their emotions rather than choosing among the alternatives that might be available right in front of their eyes. Many catastrophic blunders have been made this way. It is far better to deliberately choose a course of action in advance from the pool of possible alternative courses than blindly tromping forward to resolve family law problems.

Chances are good that you will be dealt more than your fair share of problems when you find yourself in the family court environment. After all, our court system by definition is an adversarial court system. Given the cards you have been dealt, you should logically try to resolve your family law issues the best you can. So what exactly is the family court environment?

The *family law environment* is not just limited to the actual time you and your attorney are sitting in the courtroom advocating your case or negotiating your case in chambers in front of the judge. Think of the family court environment as encompassing everything involved in the process of dealing with your family law issues. This includes everything from making key strategic decisions on how to best play your cards, all the way down to collecting old paperwork relevant to your case. The more street savvy you are in family court, the better.

THINK DEFENSIVELY

Most men never take the time to consider defense prior to an impending divorce. Once the divorce proceedings have begun, it is imperative to think defensively. Without being paranoid, it's smart to realize that someone is probably out to get you, and you probably know who that someone is—the bat from hell, of course. If your adversary isn't actually out to get you, you can rest assured that your adversary will seek to protect her best interests over yours during the divorce, regardless of the consequences to you.

Everyone who is either married or planning on getting married should have a working strategy to first avoid a divorce to begin with and then be able to deal with a divorce should it arise in the future. This is true regardless of whether or not any serious conflicts in the marital relationship have surfaced.

Going through a divorce is not a happy or easy endeavor. Wishful thinking, when unreasonable under the circumstances, can be just as hazardous to you in the family law environment as taking an overly adversarial position. Be cautious of the wild cards that might be thrown against you. Don't allow yourself to be set up by your divorcing wife. *Start thinking defense.*

If your wife has already served you divorce papers, or if blood has already been let in your relationship, like having been slapped with a restraining order, acknowledge to yourself that there's not a realistic chance of saving the marriage. Don't allow your wild emotions to let you think that the marriage is salvageable when it's obviously not. Unrealistic wishful thinking can make you a vulnerable target to the games people play.

When it's obvious *that there isn't* a reasonable possibility of reconciliation or even a desire for it, *acknowledge that reality and start planning.* Don't allow yourself to be set up for a sucker blow thanks to your being in denial of the obvious fact that the marriage is shot. Denial that a divorce is inevitable *often* makes men vulnerable targets for their scheming opponents.

RESTRAINING ORDERS

Restraining orders are quite prevalent within the family court environment. Restraining orders all have one thing in common: they order a person *not to do something.*

13

A Protection Order is one of many types of restraining orders. A Protection Order orders a person not to have any contact whatsoever with the person who is being protected by the order. *Any contact whatsoever means any contact whatsoever—period!—even through third parties.*

Protection Orders are incredibly easy to obtain and quickly enforced. Protection Orders are usually hand served by police officers to alleged aggressors within a few hours after a victim fills out a standardized fill-in-the-space application. The forms are available at County Court Administrators' Offices. Their purpose in the family law environment is to protect victims from domestic violence. Once a Protection Order has been personally served, a violation of the no-contact provision of the Protection Order is a quick ticket to jail. Violators of Protection Orders are usually dealt with harshly in criminal court.

Besides having to deal with a criminal prosecution and a stiff jail sentence, violators of Protections Orders will also see their position in divorce court *severely weakened.* Violations can destroy the possibility of a litigant obtaining either sole or joint custody over the children.

A surprising number of Protection Orders are either merit-less or fall short of the statutory grounds required for the judge to order one. They often are the result of women venting their anger. They are also maliciously obtained to gain a strategic advantage in divorce proceedings.

Another problem with Protection Orders is that because they are so widely obtained, many people who seek them are totally ignorant to the fact that there minimum statutory grounds necessary for their authorization. Not only are many of the people who seek Protection Orders ignorant of the statutory grounds to obtain them, *so too are those who are slapped with one!* If uncontested, which is usually the case; Protection Orders usually remain in place for about a year unless an extension is obtained. Chapter XV explains the ins and outs of Protection Orders in further detail.

SET REALISTIC GOALS

Your *first step* to resolve your family court issues is to set *realistic goals* for a successful outcome. *It is easy to set your goals either too high or too low.* Proper goal setting and developing effective strategies are the result of making educated decisions. *Be realistic but don't give away the farm.* A critical aspect of making informed decisions is to recognize the strengths and weaknesses of your cards as well as those of your opponent. Once you learn the critical aspects of the law in the Nutshell Chapters and apply the law to the facts of your case, you should have a pretty good sense of where you stand. Develop and use common sense strategies to put that knowledge into your best use.

DEVELOP INFORMED STRATEGIES

In the later Nutshell Chapters, you'll get a good understanding of the law and how to apply that law to the facts of your case to come up with the preferred legal outcome of your issues. That's assuming everything goes as it should in the family court environment. But things don't always go as they should in the family court environment for a variety of reasons that will be explained later.

Once you understand the preferred legal outcome of your pending divorce issues, you can use that information to develop your strategies. Your strategies in turn help you make informed decisions on the approaches to take to resolve your issues in the family court environment.

The informed decisions and the approaches you take to resolve your family law issues will help guide you and your attorney through the family law environment in the direction most likely to serve your best interests. It can help you "better play the game," as some people would state it. I prefer to think of it as "educated decision making within the family court environment." How a person plays his or her cards within the family law environment can and does play an important part in determining the outcome of family law issues, for better or worse.

15

If you take an unreasonable position on a divorce issue out of ignorance, spite, or because you are making a poker bluff that you don't have a chance in hell of winning, you will probably not only infuriate your opponent, you will probably end up irritating the judge and the other important players in your family law case as well. Such foolishness will probably hurt your credibility on your other family law issues where your cards may be good or even excellent. Such an approach will certainly hurt you and your attorney's ability to negotiate a fair settlement agreement with your opponent.

If you can come up with realistic goals and strategies that are appropriate according to your circumstances, be flexible to readjust your goals and strategies later on to deal with changing circumstances. Without being paranoid, expect the unexpected and plan accordingly. It will help give you the heads-up ability to react to any stray incoming artillery shells fired off by your opponent.

Setting realistic goals is extremely important because it determines your strategies. A man going through a divorce shouldn't blindly stumble through divorce proceedings without having realistic strategies that are adaptable to changing events.

The ability to set realistic goals when under the stress of a divorce is a lot easier said than done, due to the surreal family law environment. Don't allow your emotions to hinder you from getting into a rational business-like mode, because it will help you to more effectively meet the challenges that will confront you. Realize that your best course of action on some of your issues may include having to choose the lesser of two evils. Unfortunately, that is the nature of the beast.

When a divorce is inevitable, an atmosphere of mutual compromise makes things much easier for each side to come up with a divorce settlement that is fair and reasonable to both parties. A little give-and-take can help avoid expensive and hurtful litigation. *The key to successful negotiations is to come up with an agreement that serves both parties' best interests.*

TIME-TESTED SAYINGS

I know you have heard the expression that "history repeats itself." That saying not only applies to countries in conflict, but it also applies to people in conflict. Try to avoid the obvious pitfalls that people keep making over and over, century after century.

William Shakespeare once wrote, "Hell hath no fury like a woman scorned." Another time-tested saying states, "If you want to catch a fly, use honey, not vinegar." I have an affinity with this old saying my dad sometimes used to advise me, "Think want you want but remember to just keep your damn trap shut."

There are two other old sayings worth mentioning: "Some things should just remain unspoken", and "Be dumb like a fox."

As your keystone strategy, *your best defensive and offensive strategy is to portray yourself as being civil, polite, and reasonable regardless of what you may be legitimately feeling inside.* You can maintain your stance on the issues and still act civil, polite, and reasonable. Act the part skillfully and truly become the average Joe nice guy! I am not suggesting that that you become a pushover.

This strategy, along with *keeping your trap shut*, is a significant part of being dumb like a fox. Being dumb like a fox also means that you should proceed with the guidance of well-thought-out strategies. Acting the part of the average nice guy is a keystone strategy. Let your attorney be your aggressive advocate, but only if necessary. The only time an aggressive approach should be used in family court is when your opponent is taking an unreasonable position contrary to the preferred legal outcome of an issue.

ACT NICE EVEN IF YOU HAVE TO PRETEND

You want to come out of this situation in the best possible position. It is contrary to that basic goal if you act out of spite. A basic strategy that you should have is to act in ways to serve your best overall interests. To do that, you might have to bite your lip a few times. You don't have to sacrifice your dignity by acting respectfully—far from it. What you are doing is acting dignified. If you act disrespectful to your opponent or anyone else involved in your family law case, it will do nothing but harm your position in the family court environment.

If you want out of a relationship, then get out, but be civil about it. If she wants out, let her go. Either way, you don't have to act like an angry jerk. Men who act like angry jerks lose big time in family court. There is a line between actively defending your positions on family law issues and acting like a jerk out of spite. Knowing where the line is drawn depends on using common sense.

When you act civilly toward your disgruntled divorcing wife, it can help you tremendously to be able to formulate and negotiate a Divorce Settlement Agreement. It will also gain you favor in the eyes of the judge and the other players in involved in your case. It will favorably impress your own attorney, the opposing attorney, and even your opponent (your soon-to-be ex-wife). Being civil lessens the possibility of having your opponent turn into a full-blown bat out of hell. Acting civil and maintaining your composure is one of the ways to act dumb like a fox.

Without being pretentious, another keystone strategy that you and your attorney should have is to be fully prepared for litigation should that be necessary. This strategy is somewhat similar to Theodor Roosevelt's foreign policy statement. "Speak softly and carry a big stick; you will go far." Acting civilly along with being well prepared is actually helpful to facilitate fair settlement agreements.

DIVORCE SETTLEMENT AGREEMENTS

Your initial and continuing goal should be to try to come up with a mutual *Divorce Settlement Agreement* with your opponent that is *fair and civil* to both of you with as little pain and expense as possible. *However, never let your guard down.* Be fully prepared for a contested divorce.

Divorce settlement agreements often take time to be agreed upon. It is surprisingly common for opposing litigators to make last-minute concessions to settle divorce issues literally minutes prior to court litigation. How you present yourself, your decisions and stances on family law issues, along with your ability to be flexible and reasonable within the family court environment, makes a big difference on your ability to successfully negotiate a fair settlement agreement with your opponent. Your general demeanor, good or bad, can either soften up or embitter an opponent.

Some divorcing couples are able to resolve *all* of their divorce issues in their Divorce Settlement Agreement. *In fact, the lion's share of divorces end up using Divorce Settlement Agreements* to one degree or another. Settlement agreements can be used to resolve the divorce issues that the parties agree upon while leaving open the option to litigate any other issues they cannot agree upon. *Judges like Divorce Settlement Agreements and not-so-subtly push for them.*

Be open-minded and civil while negotiating a divorce settlement. *It involves reasonable give-and-take and compromise by both sides.* I assure you, it is *not* in your best interests to get into an ugly and expensive divorce proceeding when it could have been avoided through civil negotiations. There are different methods for the parties to negotiate a settlement. Sometimes the parties can agree upon matters between themselves. Usually, the parties' attorneys do most of the negotiations to formulate settlement agreements.

FIND A GOOD ATTORNEY

If you have any contested issues involved in your divorce, it is essential that you have an attorney represent you that you feel comfortable with. Attorneys are trained to understand the local court rules of civil procedure. Failure to follow complex court rules can be disastrous. It is important that you have an advocate and legal expert to represent and guide you. You will shortly understand the critical aspects of the law as it applies you your case, but your attorney has the means to dig deeper into specific nuances and exceptions to the general rules that may be applicable to the facts of your case.

Like any other profession, there are good attorneys and bad attorneys. Make sure that your choice is a veteran at family law and has references. Ask educated questions at your initial interview. Ask around for who is a good family law attorney. You don't want a pushover attorney, nor do you want an overly aggressive attorney. Both are equally bad. Make an informed choice. Hopefully, the information in this book will make you an informed consumer.

ALTERNATIVE DISPUTE RESOLUTION

If the negotiations with your opponent are at a standstill, Alternative Dispute Resolution may be an option you wish to explore. Alternative Dispute Resolution (ADR) is a viable and widely available option to bring the parties together in an effort to settle their family law disputes. ADR falls into two main categories, Mediation and Arbitration.

Mediation is by far the most common form of ADR used to help resolve family law disputes. Mediation is usually voluntary, but sometimes it's court ordered by the judge in an effort to get the parties to settle their differences before trial.

The first step in Mediation is for the parties to mutually agree on the mediator they wish to hire. Mediators are trained, neutral third parties who first try to help the parties identify precisely on what they can agree upon and what they disagree upon. *Then the mediator sees if the parties are able to settle their differences with a Divorce Settlement Agreement.* Mediators can help get the parties to work together to solve their problems with compromise instead of fighting each other's positions.

Mediation sessions are strictly confidential and guided by a trained mediator. The mediator lays down strict rules of conduct, which include not interrupting the other party when talking along with other rules of proper etiquette. The shared hourly expense of hiring a neutral third party mediator may well be worth the price when compared with the huge attorney fees involved in litigating an issue before the judge.

Arbitration also involves having the parties agreeing to hire a neutral third party. But unlike Mediation, *the arbitrator acts similar to a judge at a binding mini trail.*

DIVORCES CAN BE CIVILIZED

Divorces can be civilized, *even when* there is significant money and child custody issues involved. And that's the way it should be. A so-called friendly divorce can only happen if both parties are willing to negotiate reasonably and cooperatively together to come up with a fair Divorce Settlement Agreement. This can avoid expensive, time-consuming, and painful litigation and usually ends up being mutually beneficial.

It is always in the best interest of divorcing spouses to set aside their own personal greed and vendettas *for the parties' mutual benefit.* This approach becomes impossible when one or both of the parties act unreasonable, vindictive, or greedy.

Civilized divorces often occur when there are no minor children and few marital assets. After all, if there is nothing to be gained or lost through litigation, why get involved in an ugly divorce? People in this category often may be able to request do-it-yourself court forms from their local county court administrator office or from their state's online form bank, *if that is available in your jurisdiction.* Avoid national online legal form companies. If you can accomplish a friendly divorce, you should still have an attorney review the paperwork and make sure the proper court procedures are followed.

The benefit of a Mutual Divorce Settlement Agreement is obvious when there are no children or money issues involved. Believe it or not, some couples in this no-brainer category still sometimes wish to duke it out in family court just to show the world who is right and who is wrong. The only ones coming out ahead in that type of situation are the attorneys, assuming the litigants can afford to pay their attorneys.

Remember that your initial goal should be to try to come up with a fair, negotiated Divorce Settlement Agreement. Never give up that initial goal even if negotiations are not going well. At the same time, always be prepared for a contested trial. I have literally finalized divorce agreements right on the old courthouse steps just before trial.

CHAPTER 3

SLAYING THE GREEN
MONSTER

One of the hardest battles that a person has to face when going through a divorce is to face his or her own emotional demons. It's a battle you have to win for your emotional stability and self dignity.

Think about it. The only difference between a good day and a bad day *depends on a person's frame of mind* and attitude on life. A bad day doesn't depend on the weather or life's setbacks. If you are happy inside, it doesn't matter whether or not your car broke down, or whether you're behind on your payments, or faced with other common life-challenges we all face on our life's journey. Inner peace depends on whether you feel self-actualized with your life no matter what cards you are dealt. We have a very limited time on this earth; don't waste it because of the green monster.

Everyone now and again has to face his or her own negative emotions and feelings. This is especially true when going through traumatic, life-changing events. Traumatic events often make people feel like their lives are out of control.

What is the green monster? If you are human, you've faced your inner green monster before. You know what I'm talking about; I'm talking about feelings of *hurt, betrayal, jealousy, hate, injustice, damaged self-esteem, anxiety, depression, loss, hopelessness, fear, and despair.*

Defeating the green monster is easier said than done. Truly slaying the green monster is an impossible task, but you can keep it at bay.

The best we can probably do to rid ourselves of that ugly thing is to make a conscious effort to get it to crawl back into its cavernous lair to hibernate. When the glass only looks half-empty instead of half-full, it takes a deliberate effort to control one's emotions in order to regain a sense of optimism. Sometimes the only way to change a negative attitude on life is to "act the part" until you start to believe you are the character you are portraying. Doing so creates a healthy form of self-indoctrination and a self-fulfilling prophecy.

Uncontrolled, the green monster can be your worst enemy. It can lead a person on the pathway toward a *negative* self-fulfilling prophecy using *negative* self-indoctrination. Don't allow yourself to be miserable by obsessing on matters that are not currently going your way. Things always change for the better if you tackle life with a positive frame of mind. A positive attitude allows you to see each day as an opportunity to make things a little better in your life than things were the day before. The world wasn't created in a day, nor is the ability to feel self-actualized and positive about life.

The green monster is hideous. Beware. It will only hurt you. If a person allows the green monster to take over, it can lead to self-destruction, anti-social behavior, and even suicide. It often leads to abusing alcohol or drugs to cope with an overload of negativity within a person's mind. Chemical abuse is a horrible crutch that only leads to self-destruction. Don't rationalize that you are in need of temporary and necessary self-medication to get you through a bad situation that is completely out of your control. That kind of thinking is the green monster at work. Things will not get completely out of control *unless* you allow that to happen. Just remember that your inner green monster is your worst enemy and your opponent's ally.

The only thing that can slay the green monster is rational thinking. Trying to obtain clear thinking is far easier said than done. To do so you need to be as strong as you possibly can during times of emotional upheaval. Countless rehashing of negative thoughts and emotions only hurts you and robs you of the inner strength you need to defeat the green monster. It only feeds the green monster within. Alexander Graham Bell once stated, *"When one door closes another door opens; but we often look so long and so regretfully upon the closed door that we do not see the ones which open for us."*

YOUR WEAPON AGAINST THE GREEN MONSTER

That feeling of hopelessness and despair that people often feel is created by the delusion of the green monster within. *Your best weapon against the green monster is a rational, optimistic, and positive frame of mind.* A positive frame of mind allows you to make wise and rational decisions during critical periods of time when life seems hopeless. Attaining that positive frame of mind is far easier said than done when the beast has you within its grasp. Peel off that grasp, finger by finger, one negative thought after another until you are free of its grasp.

Former singer and songwriter of The Beatles, Paul McCartney, wrote a song with these lyrics: *"There will be an answer; let it be, let it be...Whisper words of wisdom; let it be."*

To forgive and forget seems like an almost unbearable task when someone has intentionally inflicted grave harm upon you. But is not an impossible task once you realize that *the person being helped by the forgiveness of another who has wronged you is yourself,* not the jerk that hurt you. It heals your soul and relieves emotional torment. Why not free yourself of self-inflicted torment?

Each time you feel a loss of self-esteem, get mad at someone else, or get angry and despair, it builds up extra baggage and clutter in your mind, piece by piece. When emotional clutter is allowed to build up too much and too fast, the excess emotional weight on your mind can blur your clarity of thought and make you feel miserable. When emotional clutter in a person's mind becomes overwhelming, it can lead to depression, aggression, and other forms of irrational thinking like

25

hateful resentment toward someone else, self-pity, and even suicidal thoughts.

It is a dangerous old wives' tale that venting one's anger is helpful emotionally because it releases it. I beg to differ. Inappropriate venting of anger only builds up extra emotional clutter partly because it makes a person look like an out-of-control jerk. *Your thoughts, deeds, and actions define who you are.* You don't need to act like an out-of-control jerk— it's counterintuitive. There is a far better way to get rid of emotional garbage. Let me explain.

Each time you can get rid of individual pieces of negative emotions like resentment, anger, and frustration from your mind, the emotional weight on your mind lifts, you feel happier, and you think more clearly. Often, the best way to lift this weight on your mind is to try to forgive and forget piece by piece or by simply letting certain matters be, and move on without rehashing it.

Some people can rely on their religion to do this. Others rely on their own vision of the Higher Power of the universe to give them the power to forgive and forget. Those that don't believe in the Almighty or their own vision of a Higher Power can simply get rid of their emotional garbage *by doing what is in their own self-interest,* which is to forgive, forget, and let it be to regain their optimism and clarity of thought.

If you feel you can't forgive, then at least try to forget it. If you aren't able to forget it, at least let it be. I'm not talking about stuffing all that emotional junk inside to resurface later on. I'm talking about *truly* forgetting it, and *truly* letting it be, once and for all.

Clarity of mind can also be gained by simply being nice to yourself. Don't beat yourself up. What possible good could come from that? You might not necessarily feel up to it, but try doing some things that make you feel happy and inspired as a means to take your mind off the countless rehashing of negativity. At least try to act like you are optimistic and satisfied with life in your daily routine. It certainly can't hurt anything, and it's better than wasting your time moping around being miserable. Don't hibernate under a rock out of fear of getting hurt again. Remember, if you play the part long enough, *you start becoming the character you are acting.* The reason why is simple: *because it's true!* After all, a person's true character and soul are defined by a person's thoughts, deeds, and actions, not by one's imagined self-image.

Acting the part until you become the optimistic person you want to be will feed your soul with positive life experiences. It will give you back that spark of positive energy you seek to regain. Having the tenacity to defeat the green monster within will enable you to get to where you want to go with life.

We often forget what is really important in our lives. For most people, it is to feel optimistic, happy, self-actualized, and most importantly to find meaning in our lives during our brief existence on this planet. You can find it in helping others and yourself. *The only difference between a good day and a bad day is simply a person's frame of mind.* Think about it. Now you know how to slay the green monster within.

CHAPTER 4

FAMILY LAW STREET SMARTS

The decisions you make now and during your family law proceedings will definitely affect your future life, both financially and emotionally. First, you must truly understand and recognize all of the cards you have been dealt, all of them—the good, the bad, and the ugly. The cards that I am referring to include the facts of your case, the law, along with the tenacity and even the morality of your opponent and her attorney. Other wild cards in the deck include the whim of your judge and the family law court system as it exists today.

If you have any minor kids with your opponent, it's possible that other players might crash the party like an appointed Guardian ad Litem representing the best interests of your children or a Child Support Officer seeking to establish and then enforce Child Support obligations.

Throughout this ordeal, you should try to be dumb like a fox. Making decisions based on wild emotions is bad news. Counter your emotions by knowing that *it is extremely important in family law that you look like the good guy*. Am I saying that you should roll over and play dead and allow the vultures and jackals to eat your carcass? No. Am I saying the best defense is an offense? No, no, *no!* What I am saying is that you must present yourself in a good light. Act nice and play your cards well using realistic and informed strategies. This approach is not only good for your soul and sense of self-worth, it will also make you feel better and strengthen your positions. Pick your battles wisely.

To be smart during a divorce is not to act like you're intelligent. Nor is it to play dumb like the fumbling actor in the old television show *Columbo*. In the show, detective Columbo always managed to cunningly outsmart the bad guy by playing completely incompetent. It gave him an edge over the bad guys because he actually was very intelligent and conniving. He used his dumb guy act as a ploy to catch the bad guys when they lowered their guards because they thought he was a fool.

To be dumb like a fox when dealing with family law matters, you have to be reserved and act according to an informed strategy without being pretentious. Don't allow yourself to be provoked into saying or doing something stupid out of spite or anger. Walk away and regroup if necessary. Play the role of the nice guy who is seeking a reasonable resolution to the case. This should be your foundational strategy. Act nice even if you feel angry inside.

When facing a divorce, the most common and often devastating pitfall is to be completely clueless as to what is going on in the family court setting while at the same time having to blindly make important and often life-changing decisions without a battle plan. Many avoidable mistakes are made this way. You should educate yourself and make informed decisions.

Don't go through this ordeal with only the blind faith that your attorney is your knight in shining armor that will save you from disaster. Sure, your attorney would like to see a favorable result for you; after all, it is difficult to get money out of disgruntled clients. Ever wonder why it's standard procedure for attorneys to require retainer fees when dealing with family law cases?

As shocking as it may sound, attorneys are usually overbooked and might not even remember you name not to mention forgetting the important facts and issues in your case until they review their jumbled notes. Don't get me wrong: there are a lot of good attorneys, and I strongly recommend that you hire a good one.

Your best defense against mediocre attorney representation is to be knowledgeable. It can also save you on attorney fees. Part of the reason why is because divorce cases often require a lot of leg work to gather important factual information like financial records, deeds, titles, and other similar information relevant to your case. You can and should do a lot of that leg work yourself. Having the proper documentation in hand to back up your claims is essential when dealing with family law issues like property distribution, alimony, and child support. Let your family law street smarts guide you to gather the *relevant* factual information you will need as ammunition for your attorney to advocate for you.

The rule, instead of the exception, is that the vast majority of family law cases have very typical family law issues. The laws regarding your family law issues are relatively easy to understand if stated in plain everyday English, instead of lengthy convoluted legalese.

The Nutshell Chapters of this book will focus on the critical aspects of the law as they relate to relevant facts of your case. The more relevant the facts are to the law that resolves an issue, the more legal weight they are given. The Nutshell Chapters will give you a sense of the *preferred legal outcome* of your family law issues together with a dash of family law street smarts. This analysis will give you a good sense of the preferred legal outcome of your family law issues.

Unfortunately, the preferred legal outcome and the real outcome don't always match due to the numerous variables within our family court environment. To better your odds, familiarize yourself with the family law environment, which includes understanding the roles and powers of other important players who become involved in your case including: your attorney, your opponent and her attorney, the judge, possibly a Guardian ad Litem and her appointed attorney, a Child Support Officer, the District Attorney, your accountant, and any other person who may become a witness for either side.

One way to put yourself one step ahead of the game is to familiarize yourself with what to expect from the other players. It gives you the heads-up on how to deal with them and how to develop effective strategies.

Most of this understanding comes naturally from your own common sense once you understand the family court environment along with the roles and the powers that the other important players have in your family court proceedings. *This common sense understanding of the family law environment and what to expect from the other players is what I refer to as family law street smarts.*

Once you understand the critical aspects of the law and what to expect in the family court environment, you have the knowledge base to develop realistic strategies targeting the circumstances of your case.

JUDICIAL WEIGHING OF FACTS

Part of understanding your current situation is to properly identify the issues and facts that are legally *relevant* to your divorce. Some of the facts of your case are more important than others. Judges give different facts different legal weights, or legal relevance, when they "weigh" the facts of a case on their imaginary "legal scale." *The legal weight of a fact on an issue depends on how relevant the fact is to answering the legal issue that is being resolved.*

The judicial weighing of the facts on the legal scale is an inexact science to say the least. Many problems can arise using this method.

All too often important relevant facts aren't presented properly (or not at all) to the judge. Many factors can tip the scale in the family court setting, including the whim of the judge. There is also a strong possibility of having biased information and even false information being introduced. It's quite OK to present the facts in an overly favorable way to one's position, but it's quite another thing to simply lie. Unfortunately, during the heat of battle, it happens all the time, in and out of court.

A prosecutor once told me that due to his long experience as a district attorney he learned how to identify false testimony being introduced during a trial. I asked him, "How's that?"

He smiled and replied, "It's when I notice the witness's lips are moving."

Another factor that can tip the scale includes *your own ability* to provide your attorney with the relevant facts of the case together with *your attorney's ability* to articulate those facts clearly when advocating for you. Make sure that you give your attorney all the facts *relevant* to the legal issue that you are facing. Doing so, it will make it easier for your attorney to present those facts to the judge as well to the opposing side during settlement negotiations.

Just like a poker game, the person with the best cards doesn't always win in divorce court, but the person with the best cards usually comes out on top. It's hard to change your cards, but you can maneuver yourself to open new avenues to play the cards you have and even acquire new cards. You have to be receptive to new opportunities and wary of the many pitfalls that can and do pop up in the family law environment.

FOCUS ON ALL THE PLAYERS

As mentioned earlier, the judge's judicial weighing of the facts is an inexact proposition because many factors can tip the scale in the family court setting. The most obvious *other factor* that can tip the scale is the input from the other important players who may have their say to the judge regarding the issues of your case.

From the very get-go, it is essential that you identify the players that have power in your case and deal with them strategically. The most obvious players are the judge, yourself, and your soon-to-be ex-wife. Even your own attorney and the opposing attorney are key players in your case. Why? That's because they all have the potential power to impact the outcome of your case.

If you have any minor children with your divorcing wife, expect that you may have to deal with a Guardian ad Litem (i.e. Court Appointed Special Advocate) if there are custody or visitation issues. Guardian ad Litems are appointed by the judge to represent the best interests of the child. They investigate the facts of a case to which they are appointed, and write a formal report to the judge on what the Guardian believes is in the best interests of the child. They even make official recommendations regarding parental custody and visitation issues along with their version of the facts that supported the Guardian's position.

Similarly, if you have any mutual children with your opponent who are under the Age of Majority, there is a good possibility that a Child Support Officer may be assigned to your case to *first* establish the amount of the child support order and *then* to enforce the order should the Non-Custodial Parent become late in paying the monthly child support obligation to the Custodial Parent.

Both the Guardian ad Litem and the Child Support Officer are supposed to be unbiased third parties who have the responsibility to make recommendations to the judge regarding child custody, visitation rights, and child support payments. It is also a well-known fact that Guardians and Child Support Officers often have a biased mindset by stereotyping men during the divorce process. They sometimes play a prosecutorial role against men who are just standing up for their legal rights.

Speaking of prosecutors, a District Prosecutor may be assigned to your case if there is an issue of late child support payments, child endangerment, or if a restraining order against you or your opponent was violated. The Guardian, the Child Support Officer, and the District Attorney and the wife's attorney sometimes even gang up together as a team to influence the outcome of a case. This result often occurs for legitimate purposes, but it can also be the result of client blunders and gender discrimination within the court system.

For Guardians and Child Support Officers, it is easier to give women preferential treatment on the issues of child custody and child support. Why? It's easier and it helps provide job security to go with the flow, and the flow is to give women preferential treatment on these issues. Your job is to try to get the other players involved in your case to go outside of their traditional course of action in family law cases in order to get them to be at least compassionate, and hopefully even supportive to your case. This is why you want to portray yourself as a nice, reasonable guy when dealing with them. It's a foundational strategy you should adopt throughout your ordeal when you deal with *anybody* in the family law environment.

A strong caveat is in order. Judges often rubber-stamp recommendations made by Guardian at Litems on child custody and visitation issues. The same is true regarding recommendations made by Child Support Officers when they help determine the amount of the monthly child support obligations that Non-Custodial Parents should pay, along with determining effective enforcement and punishment on those who fall behind in child support payments.

Although I often beg to differ on their overall expertise and competence of these so-called experts, judges rely on Guardians and Child Support Officers as experts in their fields. Their expert testimony often creates rebuttable presumptions that their recommendations are fair and equitable under the circumstances. This leaves the burden on an aggrieved litigant to overcome those presumptions with evidence to the contrary. This of course is rather difficult against these so-called experts, but quite possible because their recommendations are often questionable.

If either of these parties become involved in your case, deal with them as a likeable, average, nice guy who is trying to seek a fair resolution to your case. That is how you gain their respect. There's a strong probability they are going to be inclined to come out against you. Resist the temptation to give them a piece of your mind. Without being openly argumentative, open up windows of opportunity; inform them of facts which support you and try to logically and gentlemanly advocate your side of the story.

Do not anger or insult any of these players. You do not want them to come out gunning for you. Try to charm all the players and work with them to your advantage. Remember to be dumb like a fox when dealing with them.

Another foundational strategy is to be fully informed on the critical aspects of the law and the relevant facts of your case in order to come up with a realistic position to take on your family law issues. Judges hate parties who take unrealistic positions. It portrays ignorance and an unwillingness to take a reasonable position to resolve family law issues.

Pissing off *any* of other important players in your case will do nothing but harm you. I'm talking about *all the players* who may have an influence on the outcome of your case, including your former loving wife and her attorney from hell. Likewise, if you make a poker bluff without any cards to back you up, your bluff probably will backfire on you and only strengthen your opponent's position in court and fuel her tenacity to do battle with you.

I am not saying that you should be meek-and-mild and give away the farm. If you have legitimate grounds to make a strong stance on your family law issues, then *do so.* Reasonably advocate your position and back it up with facts and the critical aspects of the law that support your position. If litigation is necessary with an uncompromising adversary, do so, but only if you have the cards to back you up. As a guide on whether to litigate an issue, your likely benefits should outweigh your likely risks. Being shrewd without being pretentious is one of the ways of being dumb like a fox.

The only player's opinion that wins at the end of the day is that of the judge. A significant portion of this book is devoted to understanding what buttons to push and *not* to push regarding the judge. The only check and balance on a judge's vast discretionary power is to appeal the case to the state's appellate court. Appealing a case is expensive, and the probability of winning the appeal and having the case reheard is extremely low. A judge's *bad* decision alone *is not* a ground for an appeal. The judge must have made a *legal error* bad enough for it to be called either "Clearly Erroneous" or an "Abuse of Discretion" or some other high legal standard of review denoting a major screw-up going way beyond merely weighing the facts of a case poorly.

A judge's main responsibility is to be a neutral third party and apply the applicable law to the facts of a case to determine the preferred legal outcome of legal issues. Given their discretionary power, they do not always mathematically determine the outcome of a case by simply applying the law to come up with a decision. Unfortunately they sometimes determine an outcome first based on their gut feelings. A few will even resort to justifying their decision with creative interpretations of the relevant law along with subjective weighing of the facts to match their decision. It's not supposed to be that way, but it can and does happen in the family law environment, especially if a judge is biased against a litigant. I guess that's what appeals courts are for, but good luck winning an appeal based on judicial bias.

The extreme amount of fudge room allowed to judges can lead to dramatically different results in similar cases due in no small part to the way the litigants and the other players play their cards. The judge is a person no smarter than you or I. Sure, law school teaches aspiring students that the judge is supposed to be a "neutral third party" who logically (almost methodically) applies the facts of the case to the applicable law in order to come up with a fair result.

But judges are only human, and practical considerations and realities of the family law environment void the concept that there is equal justice for all. Judges are overworked, stressed for time, make mistakes, have their own biases, and very likely could give a damn about you.

Like electricity, the path of least resistance works well for judges. The judge you are facing is a state employee who is paid to do a job. Judges are stressed for time and grossly overbooked. They do not particularly like hearing the same emotion-based vague arguments over and over again, case after case. Don't confuse the judge on the points you are trying to make. Judges like presentations that are short, sweet, and to the point. Presentations to the judge should be presented in an organized businesslike manner.

Be careful when you are in the twilight zone of divorce court, because your true character and your version of the facts of the case may become irrelevant if you are made to look like the bad guy. Judges' egos, along with their extreme power and almost unlimited discretion deciding family court cases, can come out to bite the unwary and unprepared.

Remember; *act reasonable and cooperative to all the players involved in your case, especially to the judge.* I assure you that people don't call judges "Your Honor" out of any personal respect for them or because they think they are honorable. They do it because judges have vast powers over people's lives and demand respect whether they deserve it or not.

Your sense of family law street smarts should be starting to kick in a little bit. Your gut feelings should be telling you that you should play the role of a reasonable, nice guy and think before you act. Doing so will help you gain the benefit of the doubt on many matters. It will also open the other players' hearts and minds to your opinion on what is a fair resolution of your family law issues.

Keep in mind the critical aspects of the law, the relevant facts of your case, and the nature of the family law environment, and let your good old-fashioned common sense help guide you through this ordeal.

CHAPTER 5

THE MARRIAGE CONTRACT

Men contemplating marriage usually look at marriage as a mere social affirmation of a man's love and commitment to a female partner. Marriage is far more than merely a social affirmation of one's strong feelings toward someone else. *In reality, marriage is a financial contract that resolves money matters when the relationship dissolves.* So, what's love have to do with it? Nothing—legally anyway.

Once a marriage contract has been created, it creates a binding *financial contract* that can only be dissolved by a judge. It's one hell of a contract that many wish they never entered. Men planning on getting married, those married, and those currently going through a divorce should always keep the notion of damage control in the forefront of their minds.

The marriage contract is not at all like a regular contract. A regular contract is simply a legally binding agreement between two parties that agree to exchange something of value for something else of value. If one side doesn't follow the terms of a regular contract, the non-breaching party is entitled to restitution for damages due to the other side's breach of their contract. The damages given back to a non-breaching party is called "restitution" or contract damages. There's an old legal saying: "Restitution puts the non-breaching back in the same position as before the contract was breached."

TERMS OF THE MARRIAGE CONTRACT

The marital contract doesn't even consider restitution for damages due to a breach of contract. Instead, the financial issue for the judge to decide is who gets what and who pays whom according to the *unwritten terms of the contract.* The unwritten terms of the marriage contract are largely based on legal precedent and old tradition called "common law."

Marriage contracts *establish rights, benefits, and entitlements upon the termination of the marriage contract that are largely unrelated to the contractual concept of restitution* for damages.[1] You probably are becoming all too aware that the contract you bound yourself into doesn't behave according to the rules of a regular contract. It acts more like a legal partnership where the partnership property is divided up upon dissolving the partnership. But the marriage contract goes further.

Marriage contracts can also establish certain entitlement rights that may include alimony and a disproportionate split of the marital assets and debts. Whether a spouse is entitled to these entitlements depends on the facts of the case, state law, and the wide discretion of the judge when a judge decides what is fair under the circumstances.

Although child support is often ordered to be paid to the Custodial Parent during divorce proceedings, *child support is not an entitlement created by the marriage contract.* Child Support is financial obligation that depends entirely upon who sowed the seeds for the next generation. It is legally irrelevant whether the biological parents were ever married.

MODIFICATION OF THE MARRIAGE CONTRACT

In a typical contract, the contract can be changed or modified later if both parties agree to change the terms of the contract. Because the marriage contract is based on the unwritten terms of old common law, it can be modified *before* it is entered into. A change in the usual terms of the marriage contract *before a couple is married* is done with a *Prenuptial*

---

1 Many states, at least on the books, allow judges to consider marital fault as a factor in determining alimony and an unequal split of the marital assets.

Agreement. A later modification of the marriage contract after a couple is married can be accomplished with a *Postnuptial Agreement.*

The way a contract is legally created or then later modified is with the application of the basic contract principles of *offer, acceptance, and mutual consideration. Mutual consideration* is a legal concept that simply means that each party agrees to exchange something of value for something else in value.

Because the marriage contract can be modified, a modification can be used to override some of the unwanted unwritten terms of the marriage contract. *The types of common law terms that are sometimes written out of the unwritten terms of a marriage contract include the right to alimony, the right to have a judge order an unequal split of the marital assets, and spousal inheritance rights under common law. It can also change the common law notion that any income earned by either spouse is mutually owned marital income.*

The states are split on whether alimony can be waived in either a prenuptial or postnuptial modifications of the marriage contract. A few states simply prohibit enforcement of alimony waivers.

While *all states allow prenuptial agreements* to one degree or another, some states simply do not allow *postnuptial* agreements to change *any* of the unwritten terms of the marriage contract.

Prenuptial Agreements are also valuable in identifying each party's non-marital property owned prior to the marriage. Identifying non-marital property helps prevent later issues on whether a piece of property should be classified as marital or non-marital property should the marriage end in a divorce.

An attorney should be hired to draft either a prenuptial or a postnuptial agreement to ensure its validity and compliance with state law. A full and open disclosure of each party's assets and financial matters is essential to prevent a legal challenge down the road. A "mail-order" prenuptial contract may not be worth the paper it is written on.

At a minimum, all the legal elements of a valid contract must be included in these types of modification contracts (including offer, acceptance, and mutual consideration). In addition, modification contracts must also be written, mutually signed, notarized, and should even be witnessed to ensure authenticity and that the agreement was entered into voluntarily.

PRENUPTIAL AGREEMENTS

As mentioned, a couple enters into a Prenuptial Agreement *before* they are married. In a sense, a prenuptial agreement is a contract in itself in that it *modifies the rights and obligations of traditional marriage contract*. Prenuptial Agreements are useful defensive tools to help prevent future family law issues that might arise during a divorce. Prenuptial Agreements override the unwritten common law terms of the marriage contract. They can also be used to define who gets what should a divorce occur. They help limit a judge's discretionary power to divvy out the spoils of the marriage as the judge sees fit. They are useful to resolve divorce issues regarding alimony, personal income verses marital income, and property distribution.

Prenuptial agreements and postnuptial agreements are totally ineffective regarding the issues of child custody, visitation rights, and child support obligations. Child custody and visitation rights are resolved by determining "what is in the best interests of the child." Child support obligations automatically follow the person who is legally titled the Non-Custodial Parent. The amount of the obligation to be paid to the Custodial Parent is largely determined by the recommended child support obligation found in each state's Statutory Child Support Guidelines.

A *majority* of states have adopted some form of the Uniform Premarital Agreement Act (UPAA) in their state statutes. The UPAA is progressive, and it specifically allows alimony waivers in *prenuptial agreements*. Recall that a few states still do not allow alimony waivers, but all states, in principal at least, allow prenuptial agreements. The

UPAA is a definite limitation on judges' discretion to find prenuptial agreements void as against public policy or void because it encourages divorce. The UPAA specifically *lists* what prenuptial agreements can either modify or remove from the unwritten terms of the marriage contract, and the inclusive list is large.

POSTNUPTIAL AGREEMENTS

A *Postnuptial Agreement* is very similar to a Prenuptial Agreement. As its name suggests, a Postnuptial Agreement is entered into *after* a couple has already been legally married. It's a post marriage modification of the marriage contract. Both the Postnuptial Agreements and Prenuptial Agreements modify the traditional terms of the unwritten common law marriage contract. However, postnuptial agreements are not nearly as legally effective as prenuptial agreements.

Some states do not even allow Postnuptial Agreements to rewrite the unwritten terms of the marriage contract. Postnuptial Agreements are often subject to a legal attack due to a lack of "mutual financial consideration," fraud, or some other legal defect. *Prenuptial Agreements are far more effective shields* against the unwanted terms of the marriage contract than Postnuptial Agreements. Besides the fact that Postnuptial Agreements are often found ineffective and invalid, there's a chance that anyone who asks for one might end up in divorce court. It could be seen as the last straw that broke the camel's back.

ANNULMENTS

A legal annulment is a legal determination by a judge that the marriage never legally existed to begin with. The typical grounds for an annulment usually focus on the legal requirements, or lack thereof, necessary to form a valid marriage contract. *The law where the couple was married controls whether the couple entered into a legally binding marriage contract,* not where the couple is actually being divorced. Take for instance this silly example. If the law at the place where a marriage ceremony was held legally required the groom to pay the bride's family ten goats as consideration for the daughter's hand in marriage, but the groom failed to deliver the goats within the time limit, the marriage contract might fail for either a lack of mutual consideration or fraud or both.

While the statistics on the divorce rates are readily available, the statistics on legal annulments are not. Legal annulments are certainly not as common as divorces, but there are probably more cases that either *occur or could occur* than most people would imagine. A notable requirement in this country is that a person who was legally married anywhere in the world has to be legally divorced before remarrying here. There are also varying age and state residency requirements that some people fudge when applying for a marriage license. These are all valid grounds for an annulment.

The fact that a person wasn't legally divorced is perhaps the most common and easiest ground to prove for an annulment. With the current US divorce rate around 50 percent, there are a lot of separated couples who procrastinate getting a divorce for years or simply don't get divorced for a variety of reasons, including financial reasons. There are also some immigrants who come to this country without divorcing their old spouse in the old country. With computer access to public databases offered on the Internet for a small fee, finding out one's prior marital status including divorce records is not that difficult in most cases.

It's pretty much a standard legal requirement in this country to require a couple wishing to get married to buy a state marriage license and hold a marriage ceremony before someone legally authorized to marry couples as prerequisites for a legal marriage. The exception lies in a handful of states like Texas which still allow "Common Law" marriages. A common law marriage happens in those states when a couple "hold themselves out as married" over a prescribed period of time recognized by the state. So, a person who was common law married in Texas or some other country that allows Common Law marriages can't legally remarry in any state in this country without first having a divorce. After all, polygamy is illegal in this country.

There is also a problem when a person who seeks to get married is underage. This marriage can be attacked as either being fraudulent or failing the legal age requirement where the marriage occurred.

Each state also has its own residency requirements that must be met before a couple can get married in that state. Nevada is the exception in that a couple need not first reside there to get married there. This is one of the reasons why there are so many marriages in Nevada from out of state couples.

All contracts are voidable if created under undue duress or fraud. This includes marriage contracts. If a man or a woman *knowingly* enters into a voidable marriage to protect himself or herself from a divorce later on, the judge will not allow the fraudulent party to benefit from his or her fraud on the other party by allowing the case to proceed as an annulment. In this situation, the judge will require the case only proceed as a regular divorce.

RELIGIOUS ANNULMENTS

Legal annulments and church-sponsored annulments are *two very different creatures*. Church-sponsored annulments are done by religious affiliations for religious purposes only. They have absolutely no legal affect whatsoever in this country. Before a church does a church annulment, the person seeking an annulment is usually required to be legally divorced prior to requesting a religious annulment.

CHAPTER 6

FAULT VS. NO-FAULT DIVORCE

U nlike regular contracts, only judges are allowed to terminate marriage contracts. In order for a judge to have the power to legally "dissolve" a marriage, the judge must first find that there are legal "Grounds for the Divorce."

Years ago, every state required the judge to find at least one of the spouses at fault for wrecking the marriage as the ground for granting a divorce. A *majority* of states still follow this old common law rule and all allow fault-based divorces. But times have changed.

Today, the most favored method is to proceed with a divorce is with a no-fault divorce. Now, *all of the states*, even fault-based divorce states, will allow a couple to have a no-fault divorce if the judge agrees to proceed with a no-fault divorce. An increasing number of states only allow no-fault divorces.

NO-FAULT DIVORCE

In these jurisdictions, marital fault is irrelevant at least in regard to the grounds for a divorce. All that is needed in these states is to have at least one of the spouses indicate under oath that the spouses have *"an irreconcilable breakdown in the marriage."* That's it. Marital fault allegations against the other spouse are usually deemed inadmissible unless the behavior is deemed relevant to some other issue in the case. For instance, bad conduct might be relevant to child custody, visitation, or child endangerment issues. However, marital fault is openly admissible in some states, (typically in the fault based states) if a judge wishes to use it as a factor to resolve the issues of alimony and an unequal split of the marital assets.

There are significant advantages to no-fault divorces. Fault-based divorces are usually more expensive and lead to excess litigation simply because the party filing for divorce has to prove fault as the ground for the divorce. Once the mud starts slinging, more litigation often follows.

Keep in mind that statistically, the lion's share of divorcing couples resolve all their divorce issues with Divorce Settlement Agreements before their family law issues end up being litigated and resolved in court by the judge. In these types of situations, there simply is no reason to get into gut-wrenching and expensive litigation. Uncontested divorces are far cheaper and move much more quickly through the court system than those involving confrontational litigation.

Even in no-fault jurisdictions, where marital fault is usually deemed irrelevant, there's still plenty of mudslinging coming in through the back door. The reason for this is simple. Just like in politics, negative campaigning works.

In some states, the *only* option to proceed with is divorce is with a no-fault divorce. There are at least seventeen states that are strictly no-fault states and the list is growing: Arizona, California, Colorado, Florida, Hawaii, Indiana, Iowa, Kentucky, Michigan, Minnesota, Montana, Nebraska, Nevada, Oregon, Washington, Wisconsin, and Wyoming (and Washington DC).[2]

FAULT-BASED DIVORCE

Most states *allow* Fault-Based divorces. But even in all of these states, judges will proceed with a no-fault divorce if both the parties agree.

---

2 http://www.divorcesource.com/ds/divorceprocess/fault-versus-no-fault-grounds-305.shtml. The list may not be up to date.

The legal grounds for fault-based divorces range all the way from spousal abuse and adultery to impotency and incontinence—talk about throwing gasoline on the fire. As you can imagine, this situation can lead to rather ugly divorces. *So why in the world would someone these days wish to have a fault-based divorce?*

As a strategy to get more of the marital booty, many aggrieved spouses prefer proceeding with a fault-based divorce. *The reason why is because marital fault might be used as a factor in determining whether alimony or an unequal split of the marital estate is appropriate under the circumstances.* In the states that allow marital fault in the determination of alimony and an unequal split of the marital estate, it is largely up to the judge's discretion whether to do so or not.

Marital fault also shows its ugly face in resolving child custody and visitation issues in both fault-based and no-fault divorces. Pointing out bad character traits and even making up marital fault is a classic strategy many women use to gain sympathy from judges to tilt the legal scale in their favor.

Pointing out or making up marital fault is also effective strategy to gain sympathy from the other important players who may be involved in a family law case. For instance, Guardian ad Litems and Child Support Officers are often inundated with allegations of fault and bad character. This strategy applies in states that use either the fault-based or the no-fault-based approach. The reason why is because there are no effective legal limitations on what a litigant says to these other players behind closed doors. So what prevents an unethical litigant from twisting the truth out of court to one of these players in an attempt to change the outcome of the case? Nothing really; it happens all the time.

OTHER PROCEDURAL PREREQUISITES

Be aware that every state has its own procedural hoops to jump through before a divorce is granted. First of all, the states all have different *residency requirements* that must be met before the court has the jurisdiction to even hear a family law case. State residency requirements simply mean that before a spouse can file for a divorce in a state, the spouse must have lived there for a statutory period of time.

Some states also require a *"cooling off period"* of time before they will allow a divorce to proceed. This cooling off period may include living apart and separated for a number of months up to a few years. One of the advantages to a fault-based divorce is that filing for a fault-based divorce might shorten or eliminate the state's cooling off period. Your attorney should be fully aware of any procedural hoops your state requires before a divorce case can proceed.

DIVORCE RATE

Statistically over 50 percent of marriages in this country end in divorce. Along with that, at least two-thirds of divorce cases are initiated by women. Both statistics are in the realm of common knowledge. That should be a serious wake-up call. Personally, I don't believe that there are biological gender differences responsible for these dramatic statistics. These statistics are but a reflection of the common knowledge that women have a distinct advantage in the family court system.

I am convinced that because the family court system has historically women such an unfair advantage over men in divorce court in regard to every significant issue in a divorce, it actually encourages divorces. Today, prenuptial agreements can significantly reduce that advantage and, ironically, probably also reduce the number of couples who end up in divorce court.

PART II

CHAPTER 7

UNDERSTANDING THE
NUTSHELLS

T he following Nutshell Chapters give you insight to the *critical aspects of the law* that are used to determine the *preferred legal outcome* of family law disputes. Judges apply the law to the facts of a case to determine the outcome of family law issues. Often, the facts of the case support each party's position on a legal issue, at least to one degree or another. The judge is then left to decide which party's position is stronger than the other's position. This is when the judge pulls out his or her magical scale to weigh the facts of the case to determine which side should prevail on the legal issue. Some facts of course are given more legal weight than others.

Basically speaking, the more relevant a fact is to the law being used to resolve a particular family law issue, the heavier the fact will weigh on the legal scale!

A family law issue is often simply a statement of the law on an issue *made into a question.* For instance, a statement of the law on child custody states that child custody shall be determined by using the best-interests-of-the-child standard. Therefore, the legal issue is "What is in the best interests of the child?"

The following chapters provide you with the essential information you need to understand the preferred legal outcome of your family law issues. This knowledge will help guide you on your strategies. This information can also give you insight into how to intelligently and fairly negotiate with the opposing side by being better aware of the cards each side holds.

When I refer to the *preferred legal outcome of an issue*, I am referring to a best-case scenario—all the relevant facts are properly presented to the judge, no one lies, and everything comes out unbiased. The judge then methodically applies the proper aspects of the law to the relevant facts of the case to come up with a preferred resolution to a family law issue. But things don't always go that well in family court. Men have a nasty way of getting railroaded.

One of the reasons why it is important that you understand the preferred legal outcome of your family law issues is to formulate realistic strategies to face the obstacles that may confront you. It's a lot easier to deal with matters when you know what's going on, and know what the proper outcome should be.

Early in this book, I stated that "Chances are that the issues in your case are typical, and the law on your issues can be easily understood if explained in plain English. *The rule, instead of the exception, is that the vast majority of family law cases have very typical family law issues.* The law regarding your family law issues and applicable facts relevant to those issues are relatively easy to understand if stated in plain everyday English, instead of lengthy legalese."

You are probably aware that there are subtle and not-so-subtle differences in the law from state to state. On top of that, the law is slowly changing, with some states being more progressive than others. *The differences in state laws are often overemphasized. This can lead to absolute confusion. When you look closely, you will notice that the critical aspects of the law in the various states are quite similar once you consider the vast discretion judges have in all states when deciding what is fair under the circumstances.* I will try to point out some of the more important differences in the following chapters.

When you identify a legal issue that applies to your case and where the states differ in their laws on how to resolve that issue, it is imperative that your attorney advises you exactly what approach your state uses when you and your attorney formulate strategies on how to best resolve your legal issues.

When you read the following chapters, it is important that you realize that different states also use slightly different legal terminology to describe essentially the same legal concepts. For instance, most states call the property a married couple owns together *marital property*, while some states call it *community property*. Similarly, judges sometimes appoint Guardian ad Litems to represent the best interests of the child during custody disputes, while other states refer to Guardians as Court Appointed Special Advocates instead.

Unreasonable expectations by either of the litigating parties can make negotiated settlements impossible. Contested litigation is sometimes unavoidable to protect your best interests, *but only if an issue is worthy of litigation and only when you have the cards to back you.*

If you are faced with an opponent who takes an unreasonable position on an important issue when the preferred legal outcome of that issue favors your position, litigation on that issue may well be your best course of action. If so, be well prepared for the hearing; make sure your attorney is also well informed and also prepared, and let the chips fall as they may with the judge's ruling.

When trying a matter before the judge or negotiating with your opponent, it is up to you and your attorney to present facts in a manner that will ensure the judge's ruling is fair under the circumstances *to you.*

Contested litigation is not the end of the world. Use your acquired sense of family law street smarts to make informed decisions that will help you through your ordeal. Feel confident knowing that the best approach you can take is to formulate a reasonable strategy, and be reasonable and open for negotiations. Keep focused and reserved, and play the part of the nice guy. It will help you play your cards wisely in the family law environment.

I must emphasize that if you are facing *"contested"* divorce, it would be a strategic blunder not to have an attorney represent you. Your attorney is your voice, your legal counselor, your negotiator, and your courtroom paper pusher. Chances are also good your attorney is probably aware of your judge's own personal inclinations, preferences, and biases.

CHAPTER 8

MARITAL PROPERTY VS. SEPARATE PROPERTY

For better or for worse, the law considers a married couple as a single economic unit. *As a general rule, anything and everything earned and accumulated from the income of either spouse during the marriage is considered mutually owned at the time of a divorce.* Gifts given by a third party *to the couple* are also marital property. Most states call a married couple's mutually owned property *"Marital Property."* Community Property States call a married couple's property "Community Property" instead.

The property that each spouse owns individually at the time of a divorce is called *"Non-Marital Property,"* or *"Separate Property."* I will call a spouse's individually owned property Non-Marital Property instead of Separate Property simply for clarity purposes.

Don't get confused with the fact that property ownership rules *during the marriage* differ somewhat in Community Property States compared to the majority of the other states which are called Equitable Distribution States. *What's important to realize is that every state differentiates marital property from non-marital property for the purpose of dividing a divorcing couple's marital assets.*

During the divorce process, it is important to distinguish a couple's marital property from the spouses' non-marital property. Why? *Because marital property is subject to the Marital Property Division at the end of the divorce!* During the Marital Property Division, the judge orders the division according to what the judge believes is fair and just under the circumstances.

Each spouse's individually owned non-marital assets are not generally subject to the marital property division! While this is the general rule, there is a significant exception to that rule in many states. So as not to limit the judge's discretion during the division of the couple's assets, almost half of states say *that all the couple's property*, including each party's non-marital assets, should be up for grabs in the division of the Marital Estate should the couple's marital property be inadequate for a fair division of the Marital Estate.

The states that allow judges the most discretion to dig into non-marital assets for this purpose are called "all-property states" or "kitchen sink states." Others that allow a more limited use of non-marital property in the marital property division are called "hybrid states."[3]

But don't let this exception to the general rule get you lost in the details! Regardless of where you live, the general rule is that non-marital (or separate) property is not subject to the marital property division.

The exception is usually reserved for extreme circumstances when judges feel it is necessary for a fair division of the marital estate when marital assets are lacking and justice requires digging into non-marital assets. The good news is that over half of the states don't allow their judges this discretion. In the states that do, the judges should have a darn good reason for doing so.

It's the judge's job to see that *all* the property and debt that a divorcing couple owns together, called the "Marital Estate," is fully accounted for and then fairly split according to what the judge believes is fair under the circumstances.

---

3 The so-called all-property states and hybrid states include Alabama, Alaska, Arkansas, Connecticut, Hawaii, Indiana, Iowa, Kansas, Massachusetts, Michigan, Minnesota, Mississippi, Montana, New Hampshire, North and South Dakota, Ohio, Oregon, Vermont, Washington, Wisconsin, and Wyoming. See *Kitchen Sink States* - http://www.divorcesource.com/ds/encyclopedia/kitchen-sink-states-2227.shtml

There are three main issues that arise with the marital property division.

1. How do you distinguish the couple's Marital Property from each spouse's Non-Marital Property?

2. How do you distinguish the couple's Marital Debt from each spouse's Non-Marital Debt?

3. Once the Marital Property and Martial Debt are properly identified and added up into the Marital Estate, what is a fair division of the Marital Estate?

At first glance, identifying marital property seems like a simple task once one has learned the legal rules which differentiate marital property from non-marital property. But over time non-marital property often becomes commingled with marital property to one degree or another.

The result of commingling is that the property becomes part non-marital and part marital in nature. If the property is so commingled as to prevent distinguishing the non-marital part from the marital part of the property, the general rule is that judges usually classify the property as being all marital.

Once all the couple's marital property and marital debt is added up into the marital estate, the judge must enact a fair split of the marital estate. In the next chapter, you will learn the factors that judges use to split the marital estate fairly under given circumstances. These factors all have one thing in common: they help judges decide how to fairly and equitably divide the marital estate.

If an issue arises in your case as to the classification of marital versus non-marital property, your attorney can advise you if there are any exceptions to these general rules of law in your jurisdiction. It's your job to inform your attorney on the extent and the nature of your property. Keep your eyes peeled. Don't allow your non-marital property to be thrown into Marital Estate!

Equally important, make sure *that all the marital debt* is thrown into the marital estate instead of having it being assigned to you as your own personal debt! For instance, if you took out a personal loan that was used strictly for remodeling the marital home, you should argue that debt should be classified as a marital debt, not your personal debt. That argument may or may not work with your judge. Regardless, the judge should add that as a factor on the legal scale when determining a fair and equitable split of the marital estate.

As a general rule, personal debt like student loans or personal credit card debt is classified as personal debt in *most* states, not the debt of the marital estate. However, you will note later that some Community Property states believe that all debt acquired during the marriage is Marital Debt, even if it's personal credit card debt. But even in most of these states, the judge has the discretionary power to assign it as personal debt.

MARITAL PROPERTY

Any property accumulated during the marriage from the *income* of either spouse is marital property. *Income* is the key word. *The general rule in all states is that income from either spouse is marital income. Any property purchased from marital income is therefore a marital asset.* This is true even if only one spouse has title on the property. However, properly drafted prenuptial agreements can shield a spouse's income from being classified as marital income.

Marital property can literally include anything that has a dollar value that was *either earned or gifted to the couple* during the marital partnership. This can include money in the bank, stocks, bonds, individual pensions, individual retirement accounts, vested life insurance balances, real estate, personal property, and any other imaginable asset. A business can also be classified as a marital asset as well as the blue-sky customer base of that business.

Unjust as it may be, even some forms of future disability income and cash awards for personal injury can be classified as a current *marital asset* (but not pain and suffering)—at least in a few states. This is based on a ridiculous theory that future disability income, *if earned during the marriage*, is a current marital asset. However, under federal law, future military disability income cannot be classified as a current marital asset.

A minority of states (e.g. New York) *even* allow a spouse to have a financial interest in the value of the other spouse's educational degree and professional license if acquired during the marriage! I don't know whether to laugh or cry or scream, "Involuntary Servitude!"

Thankfully, a spouse's *future* Social Security benefits and *future* Social Security Disability Income *cannot be classified as* current marital asset due to the Social Security Act. However, the other spouse does have the right to *Spousal Social Security Benefits* if qualified according to Social Security rules (which require at least ten years of marriage, along with the requirement that the person seeking Spousal Social Security has not remarried). Don't worry about Spousal Social Security Benefits because they have no impact on your own Social Security Benefits.

The bottom line is that your *own* future Social Security Benefits will not be split as a current asset in the division of the marital estate. However, as you will see later, Social Security Retirement Benefits and Military Disability Benefits can be garnished for *child support.*

Individual retirement accounts and individual pensions earned during the marriage are classified as marital property. However, any portion of any retirement accounts (401k and IRA accounts included) or pensions earned *prior* to the marriage or after a legal separation are classified as *non-marital property.* An accountant can be very useful for distinguishing which part of the retirement account is non-marital and which part is marital using these principals of law. The passive increase in value during the marriage of non-marital property is generally considered non-marital while the income is generally considered marital in nature.

Don't allow your non-marital portion of these accounts to be classified as marital property just because you and your attorney didn't do the leg work to provide the proper paperwork to the judge and the opposing side during settlement negotiations.

NON-MARITAL PROPERTY

Non-marital property, which is often called "separate property," is a spouse's individually owned property. *The general rule is that non-marital property is not subject to the division of the marital estate.*

While most states do not allow judges to split non-marital property in the divisions of the Marital Estate, there is a significant exception to this general rule. As just mentioned, almost half of the states *do* allow judges discretionary power to bend this general rule and dig into non-marital property when judges feel it is necessary in order to make a fair and equitable division of the Marital Estate. *Do not allow this exception to the general rule confuse you or diminish your right to advocate that what is yours is yours.* Even in All-Property states, it is extremely important to distinguish marital property from non-marital property. At the end of the day, the judges in these states usually put great weight on the justice scale in deference to a person's individually owned separate property.

Non-marital property is defined as property accumulated by either spouse either prior to the marriage or given to an individual spouse as a gift or an inheritance during the marriage. Recall that gifts *to the couple* are classified as marital property, not non-marital property.

If a property is purchased during the marriage using non-marital funds, should that property be classified as non-marital property? Generally speaking, the answer to that question is *yes*. However, if there is a dispute as to the nature of the property, there can be tracing problems as to whether the property was actually purchased with non-marital assets. Another issue that can arise is whether a piece of property purchased using non-marital assets was *intended* to be either a *gift* to the couple or a gift to the other spouse, or whether the property was *intended* to remain no-marital in nature. Any non-marital asset gifted to the couple by one of the spouses makes the property marital property. The same is generally true if one spouse gifted a non-marital asset to the other spouse during the marriage. Generally speaking, any non-marital property gifted to the other spouse during the marriage is classified as marital property.

Remember, some of the assets you accumulate individually *during the marriage* are non-marital assets. You might have bought an asset during the marriage using your non-marital assets. The non-marital nature of the asset remains if that was your intent, but you might have the burden of proving it was intended to remain non-marital in nature if it is contested as being marital property by the other side.

You might have been *personally gifted* grandpa's model-T when he was alive. You might have *personally inherited* the family farm while you were married. These are clearly non-marital assets *because gifts given exclusively to a spouse by a third party are always classified as non-marital property, even if received during the marriage.*

Premarital engagement rings and wedding rings exchanged at a marriage ceremony that are given to the other spouse are non-marital assets once a couple is married. Most states however consider engagement rings as conditional gifts owned by the gifter if a marriage is called off.

The general rule is that *gifts given by one spouse to the other spouse during the marriage* are *considered marital property.* That expensive diamond necklace, that ten-thousand-dollar certificate of deposit, that cabin in the woods, that fancy new car you gave her last year, or any other gift you gave her *while you were married* might turn out to be half yours in the marital property division, because gifts from one spouse to the other spouse are generally seen as marital property.

COMMINGLED PROPERTY

As mentioned earlier, if non-marital property is commingled with marital property, the result is that the property becomes part marital and non-marital in nature. This can lead to accounting problems, especially if there isn't proper paperwork and the couple doesn't agree on the nature of the property. If this has happens to you, do the leg work to provide the paperwork that your attorney can show as evidence to the judge. Consider using an accountant to provide clear documentation on commingled property. If both spouses agree on the nature of the commingled property, the judge will usually agree on the couple's classification of the property.

Recall that the general rule is that when a non-marital asset is overly commingled with marital assets through the years as to make it impossible to differentiate which part of the property is martial and which part of it is non-marital, the judge will likely find the property to be *all marital* in nature, absent of course an agreement by both spouses as to the nature of the property.

If title on a piece of property has each spouse's name on it, the property will be classified as a marital property regardless if it was purchased with non-marital money. It will be seen as a gift to the couple.

A property that has only one spouse's name on the title will be classified as marital property during the divorce if the property was purchased using either marital property or marital income. That fancy pickup you may have purchased using your own income during the marriage is a marital asset regardless if the title only has your name on it at the time of a divorce. *Your* income during the marriage is marital income, and anything you buy with marital income is a marital asset.

NON-MARITAL ASSET APPRECIATION AND INCOME

The appreciation in value (*due to passive inflation and market influences*) on non-marital property during the marriage is generally classified as *non-marital* in nature unless the increase in value is attributed an investment of marital money or due to the "sweat equity" involving the labor of either spouse during the marriage. *This is a very important and often overlooked general rule of law! All too often, the increase in value of a non-marital asset is wrongly classified as marital income (profit).*

However, some states do consider the passive increase in value of non-marital property from inflation as being marital in nature. If this is an issue in your case, your attorney should research how you state deals with the passive increases in value of non-marital assets. It is easy to confuse this point of law because any *income* from non-marital assets should be distinguished from an inflationary increase in value.

The *general rule in most states is that* <u>income</u> *from non-marital property* (like interest income or rental income) is considered *marital income.* However, a very small minority of community property states and some other states believe that the income from non-marital property should remain non-marital in nature. If non-marital asset appreciation and asset income are issues in your case, your attorney should research this matter to find out where your state stands on these issues.

MARITAL PROPERTY PRESUMPTION

What happens when a piece of property is disputed as to whether it is marital or non-marital in nature? When such an issue arises, *it creates a rebuttable presumption that the property is marital in nature unless it is shown to the satisfaction to the judge that the property is non-marital property.* The burden of proof is on the person claiming that the property in question is non-marital. This resolves the classic "he said, she said" situation. Translated: she wins unless you can prove she is lying.

For instance, a personal gift to *one* of the spouses during the marriage from a third party is clearly a non-marital asset. If the other spouse claims it was a gift to the couple, the property will be classified as a marital asset unless the spouse who was gifted the asset can prove that it was a personal gift. This may be difficult or impossible if the person who made the gift has died. Even if the person who gave the gift is alive

63

and testifies that the gift was an exclusive gift to one of the spouses, the judge may disagree and make a finding of fact that the gift was to the couple and therefore marital in nature.

The marital property presumption is also commonly used to resolve issues regarding commingled property. This presumption shifts the burden of proof onto the person claiming that the property is part non-marital in nature. Without adequate proof to the contrary, this presumption will result in the whole property being classified as a marital asset.

So what does it mean that the marital property presumption can be rebutted by a "preponderance of the evidence" to the contrary? When someone rebuts something, it means that it is disproven. A "preponderance of the evidence" simply means that the person contesting that an asset is non-marital in nature has to provide enough evidence to the judge to convince the judge that there is over a 50 percent likelihood that the asset is non-marital in nature. If a presumption arises against your non-marital property, it is up to *you* to find and provide evidence, like old paperwork or witnesses, for your attorney to use as ammunition to rebut the presumption.

In many Community Property States, there is a *strong* automatic presumption that *anything* purchased during the marriage is marital property. This confuses many because that presumption is also rebuttable. However, the standard of proof needed in these states to rebut that presumption is with "Clear and Convincing" evidence. This is a far higher standard of proof than simply the "more likely than not" standard of proof. Written proof at the time of purchase showing intent that a property remains non-marital in nature may be required to overcome this threshold. Anyone purchasing significant assets during a marriage using non-marital assets should make a paper trail showing intent that the property should remain non-marital.

If possible, a simple written statement or agreement between the parties identifying and dividing the party's marital and non-marital property is the best way to avoid litigation on the division of the marital estate. A little give-and-take can go a long way when these types of issues arise.

THE MARITAL ESTATE

The marital estate of a divorcing couple is simply the combination all the marital property the couple owns along with all the marital debts the couple owes. It can be summarized in a balance sheet with opposing assets and liabilities to come up with the couple's net worth (or negative net worth should that be the case).

CHAPTER 9

THE MARITAL ESTATE DIVISION

Almost all states explicitly allow judges to order an unequal split of the marital assets when they believe the facts of a case warrant it. A few Community Property States try to be more standardized and say that there should be a fifty-fifty split of the marital assets unless there has been a fraudulent "wasting" of marital assets by one of the spouses. Some states set up a "rebuttable presumption" of a fifty-fifty split and define certain factual circumstances which can rebut that presumption.

The fifty-fifty approach puts more limits on the judge's discretion to split marital assets unequally. Don't despair. The methods used by the states are far more similar than dissimilar. The extremes on either side have the same goal. That goal is to split the divorcing couple's assets and liabilities fairly under the circumstances.

Keep in mind what motivates judges; they want to make a fair split of everything that a couple owns together. It is also their job to make sure that the spouses keep their individually owned property separate from the split of the marital estate.[4]

Just like judges have a sense of what is fair under the circumstances, you and everyone else has that same sense of what is fair and what is not fair. If you and your opponent are at odds on splitting the marital estate, it's up to you and your attorney to properly present the relevant facts in

---

4 Recall that a significant minority of states allow judges to dip into a spouse's non-marital assets if the marital assets are inadequate to make a fair split of the Marital Estate. The all-property states and the hybrid states are listed on page 56.

your case that will incline your judge to order a larger piece of that pie to you. Knowing what factors in your case will incline a judge to favor your position is vital when negotiating a fair and reasonable property settlement agreement with your opponent.

Flexible arrangements are often used to divide the assets and the debts of the marital estate. This approach allows a lot of negotiating room for the parties to avoid tax consequences and the loss in value of certain properties which can occur during a forced liquidation. The husband might seek to keep the family business assets intact and run that business while the wife may seek more liquid assets or the family house.

EQUITABLE FACTORS USED TO DIVIDE THE MARITAL ESTATE

There are no exact formulas with the equitable approach to dividing the marital estate. An off-the-record but *common sense* approach for a judge to start with is to assume a fifty-fifty split of the marital estate and adjust that split if the facts warrant an unequal split. *Some states actually use this method on the record as a presumption* in their state laws, including many of the Community Property states.

There are many common sense factors which can influence a judge's decision on dividing the marital estate. For instance, how long was the marriage? A gold digger married for a short amount of time doesn't have the same equitable rights as a longtime spouse would. That would obviously be unfair and contrary to common sense.

Did one spouse miss out on a possible career by assuming all the childrearing and homemaking duties? Did a spouse support the career of the other spouse? Does either spouse have a physical or mental disability? Does the custodial parent need the family home and other assets like the family van to help bus the children? What are each of the spouse's non-marital assets and non-marital liabilities? What are the relative income potentials of each spouse? What was each of the spouse's relative financial contributions to the marital assets?

Just look for any relevant facts in your case that could influence a judge's decision either way on how to divvy up the marital estate most fairly. These are the same factors that should be used when negotiating a settlement agreement with the opposing side. When both parties are openly aware of the facts that will influence a judge's decision, it can help soften up both sides to try to avoid needless litigation.

In some fault-based divorce jurisdictions, marital fault is openly allowed as a factor for the judge's consideration in dividing the marital estate. By contrast, in no-fault divorce jurisdictions, fault is technically irrelevant in the divorce proceedings at least in regard to the grounds for a divorce. But I assure you that even in the no-fault jurisdictions where marital fault is probably deemed irrelevant; fault can come in through the back door to influence the judge on the Marital Property Division.

COMMUNITY PROPERTY STATES

The states which are classified as Community Property states are Arizona, California, Idaho, Louisiana, Nevada, New Mexico, Texas, Washington, and Wisconsin. Puerto Rico is a community property territory. Alaska allows a couple to opt-in into the community property system.

These states adopt the position that *during a marriage* each spouse owns the couple's community property and debt equally. This affects issues relating to ownership, transfer, and even income taxes *during the marriage*. This is the reason why a lot of people get confused about how these states handle the division of the marital estate. There is no reason for confusion. *When it comes down to a divorce, community property states use a similar approach as all other equitable distribution states— to divide fairly under the circumstances what the couple owns together and to assign each its own separate property.*

While no two community property states are identical, one of the most important differences between these states and other states are the partial limitations on judges' discretion during the division of the marital estate. California, Nevada, and Louisiana start out with the premise of the rigid fifty-fifty rule in the division of the marital estate and then give *limited* factors that judges can use to change the fifty-fifty presumption. The other community property states give the judges more room to wiggle in varying degrees all the way to the other end of the spectrum, which allows judges a wide discretion in an equitable distribution of the marital estate. For instance, Texas allows an unequal distribution of the marital estate and even allows judges to use marital fault as a factor in deciding an equitable distribution of the couple's community property.

An excellent description of the equitable factors each state uses to modify the fifty-fifty rule in Community Property States was done by CreditCards.com called "Community Property Laws by State," by Tyler Metzger and Marcia Frellick.[5] Listed on this website are the factors that each state currently can use to make an unequal split of a couple's community property.

There are other noteworthy differences in some of these states. Most, but not all, Community Property Sates believe that the *income from non-marital property (called "separate property") should be classified as non-marital property.* Recall that *most* states consider the income from non-marital property as marital income. You can also note from that website that debt acquired during the marriage is distributed *equally* in the Community Property states of California, Nevada, and Louisiana. This can lead to the problem of having personal debt, including personal credit card debt, being unfairly put into the marital estate as a marital debt.

PROPERY SETTLEMENT AGREEMENTS

Ideally, it always best to come to an agreement with your divorcing spouse on the nature of the marital estate and how it should be divided. Even when the parties can agree on most of the marital property assets and division, a judge may have to decide the proper classification and division on the more controversial assets like commingled assets, retirement income from pensions or 401k's, or future disability income. Yes, believe it or not, future retirement income and disability income is

5 *www.creditcards.com › Credit Card News* You +1'd this publicly. Mar 22, 2011

often classified as a current asset rather than future income. Say what? Somehow that doesn't pass the sniff test on my sense of what is fair. What sense is there in taking away a disabled person's future disability income?

Don't squabble over insignificant assets like worn-out household furnishings and the toaster unless you want to piss off your divorcing spouse and the judge.

The key to successful negotiations often hinges on providing an agreement that is in the mutual best interests of both parties. It is also beneficial to have both opposing sides be fully aware on the likely way a judge would rule on the matter if it was litigated.

When dividing the marital estate, it is in the mutual best interest of the parties to avoid capital gains taxes, which can occur when the judge liquidates any assets that have increased in value. For instance, there are rules in the tax code that eliminate any capital gains on the marital home if held long enough by at least one of the spouses. Selling an asset like farmland which has significantly increased in value can cost thousands of dollars in capital gains taxes. Unnecessary tax consequences can be avoided with proper planning and tax consultation.

A couple may also decide not to liquidate a business or a real estate holding due to a desire to prevent the loss of future income on that piece of property or business.

FIND THE PAPERWORK

Be sure to provide your attorney with all of your relevant legal paperwork like Deeds, Titles, Wills, Bank Accounts, Stocks, Bonds, Income Tax Filings, and the like. If your opponent is in possession of these documents, consider a formal discovery "Request for Documents." If you have significant assets at issue, have your accountant list, add up, and summarize the Marital Assets and Marital Debts along with Non-Marital Assets and Non-Marital Debts. An organized written summary of this sort makes your presentation to the judge easier to understand. *If a judge doesn't understand the presentation of the facts, the presentation is worthless. Make it as easy as possible for the judge and the opposing side to understand the nature of the marital estate along with your non-marital assets.*

Men often get stuck with most of the marital debts along with some of the other side's non-marital debts simply because they weren't identified and documented properly. Like marital assets, marital debts are subject to the division of the Marital Estate because they are a factor in determining the net value of the Marital Estate.

I would much rather pay my accountant to provide the documentation of my non-marital and marital assets than an expensive attorney. Judges also consider accountants expert witnesses who are less likely to be biased.

If real estate is owned in another state, be aware that the rules on the division of that real estate might be influenced by the law in the state where the real estate is located if the law there is somehow different. This is especially true when one state is a community property state and the other is an equitable distribution state. For instance, the other state may be a community property state that classifies *income from non-marital property as a non-marital asset,* while your state may follow the majority rule that *any* income during the marriage is classified as marital income. Recall that most states consider an increase in value of a non-marital asset through passive inflation remains non-marital in nature, but some states disagree and classify it as a marital asset. If a sizable marital asset is located in a community property state, it may also be better shielded from an unequal split of the marital estate compared to equitable distribution states.

Men often get screwed by the Marital Property Division because they and their attorneys don't submit the paperwork in an easy-to-understand way. It can happen to commingled property, like retirement accounts and real estate. It can happen on non-marital property which increases in value due to inflation. The inflationary increase in value of a non-marital property might be wrongfully classified as a marital income instead of just an inflationary increase in value of a non-marital asset.

Also, not-so-subtle gender discrimination is at work—illegal as it may be. If you get into a dispute without any hard evidence, guess who is more likely to sway the judge. Get your documentation in order if you have any assets that might be at issue, along with any debts.

WASTING MARITAL ASSETS

The wasting of marital assets refers to marital misconduct that wastes or unfairly depletes marital assets. Gambling away marital money or burning down the marital home out of spite are both extreme examples. I heard about a guy that supposedly chain sawed the marital home in half with a chain saw after hearing the house was to be divided.

Far less extreme forms of misconduct may be construed as wasting of marital assets. For instance, a spouse using marital assets strictly for his or her own purposes during a divorce can be seen as wasting of marital assets. An overly speculative investments during the marriage might be seen as wasting marital assets. When a judge believes a spouse has wasted marital assets, the result is that the other spouse will probably receive a proportionally larger share of the marital estate.

After reflecting on the facts of your case regarding marital assets and debts, what is you sense of fairness regarding a split of your Marital Estate? Are there assets you own that should be declared as non-marital assets? Be willing to compromise with your opponent. Talk to your accountant about possible tax implications and alternative solutions. Get your paperwork together as evidence on all these matters and get that documentation to your attorney in an organized manner.

If you get an unfair ruling in the Division of the Marital Estate, you cannot later motion the judge to change the ruling, due to the "finality rule." The finality rule applies to all rulings regarding the division of the marital estate, right or wrong. Unlike many of the other issues in family law which can be raised later due to Changed Circumstances, the finality rule states that all rulings on the division of the marital estate are final, period.

Your only recourse is to appeal an unfair marital property ruling to your state's appellate court. There are strict time limits on any appeals. An appeal usually has to be served within about ninety days after the order has been served on the parties from the courthouse. Appeals are expensive, and the chances are slim for a reversal, especially on family law matters. Your only realistic chance for success on all of your divorce issues is to do it right the first time.

CUT THE STRINGS

If you have physically moved from your residence, make sure your phone number and mailing address are changed. This is often overlooked at the beginning phases of a divorce. You do not want your mail or personal phone calls being monitored. Also, have *any joint* lines of credit or credit cards canceled immediately so your opponent doesn't rack up debt in your name.

But, if you have any joint checking or saving accounts, be careful and seek legal advice on how to proceed. You may need an agreement with your opponent, or authorization from the judge to access that money if the money is marital in nature.

If you close out a joint checking account or savings account and take all the money and hide it, you're looking for big trouble with your divorcing spouse and the judge. The same advice applies to changing the locks on the marital residence—even if you are living there alone. You cannot exclude your spouse's right to enter the marital residence unless the judge grants you full temporary possession of the residence, or if you have a restraining order against your spouse not to enter the residence. You do not want to break any state laws or be in violation of any fine print in a court order. These are avoidable traps that many fall into. Always think of the likely consequences before you act.

CHAPTER 10

ALIMONY A.K.A. MAINTENANCE

N ot so subtle gender discrimination against men is still alive and well in the court system regarding the issue of alimony. It's newsworthy to hear of a man being awarded alimony against his ex-wife (unless of course the ex-wife is a wealthy strung-out celebrity). Besides the issue of discrimination in the application of the law, alimony is arguably unconstitutional under the Involuntary Servitude Clause of the Thirteenth Amendment. It's only a matter of time until the guys and gals in the black robes on the Supreme Court admit it, but it will probably take another generation or two.

The Thirteenth Amendment forbids citizens from being forced to work against their will solely for someone else's benefit. From Section I: "Neither slavery nor involuntary servitude, except as a punishment for crime whereof the party shall have been duly convicted, shall exist within the United States, or any place subject to their jurisdiction."

The foundation of alimony is crumbling and becoming increasingly disfavored. But it is still present in the family court environment. It would be foolish to counterattack an alimony claim based on the fact that it is unconstitutional. Many have tried and failed. To attack an alimony claim, attack it where it is most vulnerable: *by arguing that an alimony order would be unjust and unnecessary according to the facts of your case.*

Alimony is a very old concept adopted from English law hundreds of years ago. Back then, divorced women had little income potential and usually had a "reasonable need" for alimony income to simply survive. Developed long before social security, child support, and social welfare programs, it helped finance a social net for divorced women and their children.

There simply isn't any current rationale for awarding alimony these days other than it is been around for years. State laws are increasingly limiting its use, and judges are becoming increasingly reluctant to order it.

LEGAL ISSUE

The legal issue for the judge to decide when a party makes a claim for alimony is to determine *whether the party asking for alimony has a "reasonable need or a reasonable expectation" for spousal support due to the former marriage, and if so, whether the former spouse has the financial means to maintain that lifestyle for the other spouse.*

Like all areas of family law, judges have had vast discretion when deciding to award alimony claims. Judicial discretion can lead to dramatically different interpretations of the definition of what is a "reasonable need" to maintain a lifestyle afforded by the former marriage. Interpretations can range from mere subsistence and job training, all the way to maintaining a lavish standard of living that the marriage previously offered. The length of an alimony award can be short or all the way 'until death do you part.'

An obvious defense against an alimony claim is that the person requesting alimony doesn't have a "reasonable need" and should have to work for a living like everyone else. Another defense against an alimony claim is that an alimony obligation would create an undue financial burden on the party having to make the payments.

Defenses against an alimony claim include an inability to pay for alimony due to ongoing child support obligations, financial liabilities, age, insufficient income, disability, short length of marriage, and so on. Prenuptial Agreements can also shield a person from an alimony claim, at least in most states. A small minority of states say the right to a possible future alimony award cannot be waived in a prenuptial agreement. But an alimony award is purely up to the judge's discretion, and having a prenuptial waiver might influence a judge not to grant alimony even in the states that technically don't allow alimony waivers.

FAIR UNDER THE CIRCUMSTANCES

When a judge is entertaining an alimony claim, along with the amount and length of an alimony award, the judge has to decide whether an order would be *fair under the circumstances*. This is the same consideration that judges use when deciding whether to award an unequal split in the couple's marital property. In fact, many of the same fairness factors that are used to determine an equitable division of the marital estate are also used in determining whether an alimony reward is fair under the circumstances.

Some states openly allow judges to consider marital fault as a factor when determining whether to award alimony. It's totally up to a judge's discretion to do so in those states. Even in states that don't allow marital fault as a factor when determining alimony, judges often come down hard on bad actors anyway.

A woman seeking alimony has the best chance of receiving an order for alimony if there is a wide disparity regarding the party's income potential along with a long marriage. Extra consideration will be given to a spouse requesting alimony who forwent his or her own education and career goals to support the couple while the other spouse was enrolled in higher education and career advancement. Once again, judges balance the facts on both sides.

Another significant consideration is whether the party seeking alimony made significant, *lengthy nonfinancial contributions* to the partners' standard of living, like providing for the children and home-keeping duties. Weight on the legal scales will also be given to a party seeking alimony if the party doing so is disabled or otherwise unable to make a sustainable income.

Long-term alimony awards are unlikely unless at least some of *the above significant factual circumstances regarding an alimony award* apply to the facts of the case. Alimony is not an automatic benefit. *The shorter the marriage, the less likely a judge will order alimony.*

Spousal fault for causing a divorce, whether on record in fault-based jurisdictions or off the record in no-fault jurisdictions, is another factor that can tip the scale on whether an alimony award is reasonable under the circumstances.

DURATION OF ALIMONY OBLIGATIONS

Judges have wide discretion on the duration of alimony orders. But, some states have statutory restrictions on the length and amount of alimony awards! Short alimony awards that last *only* for the duration of the divorce are called "temporary alimony" orders.

By contrast, *Final Alimony* awards are awarded at the end of the divorce in the Final Divorce Decree. *Final Alimony awards can be for a short set period of time (in months or years) all the way to a Permanent Alimony Order.*

The length of an alimony award is influenced by the length of the marriage and other equitable factors. The standard the judge uses is whether an alimony award would be fair under the circumstances.

ALIMONY ENDS WHEN THE RECIPIENT REMARRIES

If alimony is awarded, *the obligation to make alimony payments ends upon the remarriage of the ex-spouse who is receiving alimony.* There are of course some recipients receiving alimony payments who try to get around this general rule by simply not getting married to a new partner.

To discourage this type of fraud, some states have extended this general rule to include cohabitation of the ex-spouse with a significant other. In states that have not extended the general rule, the payer of alimony still has a right to file a motion for "changed circumstances" in an attempt to either reduce or eliminate the alimony obligation. After all, when an ex-spouse shacks-up with a significant other, they have two incomes to live on rather than just one income.

ALIMONY ENDS IF EITHER THE RECIPIENT OR PAYER DIES

The general rule is that the obligation to make alimony payments ends upon the death of either former spouse. However, some states allow the person receiving alimony to make a claim on the payer's estate after his or her death. -So much for the vow that "until death do you part."

INCOME TAXES

The tax code regards alimony as *"ordinary income" for the person* receiving the payments and as a tax deduction to the person making the payments. Unlike alimony, the person receiving child support payments is not taxed, and the payer of child support gets no income tax deduction on the money spent for child support.

CHANGED CIRCUMSTANCES

An alimony award can be modified or terminated in a motion hearing for "changed circumstances." The grounds for changed circumstances include remarriage or cohabitation of the recipient, death of either party, or a significant financial change in circumstances.

There are of course procedural hoops required for filing any motion hearing for changed circumstances. The standard waiting period since the matter was last heard obviously do not apply if the spouse receiving alimony remarries or either party dies.

The grounds for motioning a judge to reduce or eliminate an alimony award due to a financial change in circumstances are similar to the grounds for a party asking the court for a reduction of child support. There has to be a *substantial change in circumstances,* and the change must *not have been caused in bad faith.* For instance, a reduction in alimony payments may be motioned for due to job loss, a new disability, and other similar predicaments that might have created substantially changed circumstances since the judge ordered the alimony award. Intentional underemployment is considered bad faith and, therefore, precludes a modification of alimony due to a change in financial circumstances.

Alimony is a controversial topic and politically risky for a judge handing out too many questionable alimony awards. After all, a family court judge is merely an attorney turned into an elected politician. The bad news is that women are increasingly seeking and receiving temporary orders for alimony by obtaining questionable and even fraudulently obtained restraining orders.

Unlike child support, which is guaranteed to be awarded to the Custodial Parent who was awarded "physical custody" when parentage has been established, alimony is far from a guaranteed entitlement. Still, it's pretty much standard procedure for women's divorce attorneys to ask for alimony, even when the facts obviously suggest that an alimony award would be highly unlikely. Simply put, it's a good strategy for women to play the alimony card. It's a bargaining chip that can be used in settlement agreements. After all, women have absolutely nothing to lose by playing the alimony card and potentially a lot to gain.

STATUTORY LIMITS ON ALIMONY

If an alimony award is a possibility in your case, it is imperative that you and your attorney are aware of any legal restrictions your state has adopted to limit alimony awards! The laws are changing. For instance, some states require that a couple must have been married for at least ten years before a judge can award alimony. *Some states even have written laws in their statutes restricting the amount and length of alimony awards.*

CHAPTER 11

CHILD CUSTODY AND
VISITATION

hild Custody and Visitation issues are resolved by answering a
simple question: *"what is in the best interests of the child?"* The
factors used to resolve these issues are quite different from those used to
resolve the marital property division and alimony awards. The focus here
is not on the rights of the parents; the focus is on how to best promote the
emotional and physical well-being of the child.

PHYSICAL CUSTODY VS. LEGAL CUSTODY

"Physical Child Custody" and "Legal Child Custody" have two very
different legal definitions. Physical child custody, as the name suggests, is
the legal right to have actual physical control of the child, which includes
having the child live at the Physical Custodial Parent's residence. Legal
child custody refers to the right to make parental decisions for the child
including educational decisions, medical decisions, choice of religious
upbringing, and other similar decisions parents typically make.

PHYSICAL CHILD CUSTODY

Physical Child Custody is the term describing the legal rights and
obligations a parent is awarded by a judge to raise and house a child.
In typical divorce, one of the biological parents (usually the mother) is

ordered to have sole Physical Custody over a child, and the other parent is ordered to have Reasonable Visitation. The parent awarded sole Physical Child Custody is called the *"Custodial Parent."* The parent left without any physical child custody rights is called the *"Noncustodial Parent."*

Physical Child Custody can be awarded to *both* parents. This is called *"Joint Physical Custody."* Each joint custodial parent is assigned "Parenting Time" within a calendar year. The amount of Parenting Time assigned to each joint custodial parent can vary from a fifty-fifty split to some other relative fraction of the year or years.

Although used in a minority of custody cases and shunned by many women's advocates, Joint Physical Custody is becoming increasingly more common. Ideally, and even in reality as shown by statistics, having a real parental relationship with both biological parents is usually in the best interests of the child. In recognition of this fact, a majority of states have even placed either a rebuttable presumption or a statement of preference favoring "joint custody."[6] However, "there is a great deal of murkiness about what is meant by the term "joint custody" as it is used in the 50 states and the District of Columbia. In some jurisdictions, "joint custody" may include physical custody, explicitly or implicitly; in others, it may have the more narrow meaning of "joint legal custody."[7]

A significant entitlement that Custodial Parents have is the right to receive child support from the Noncustodial Parent. This benefit is often neutralized when the parents share Joint Physical Custody. In chapter 13 we will explore the details of child support along with the other financial obligations that Noncustodial Parents are often ordered to pay Custodial Parents.

---

6 The ANCPR, The Alliance for Non-Custodial Parents Rights is an excellent reference linking statutory and case law precedent in thirty-five states that have rebuttable presumptions or statements of preference for joint custody over sole custody. *Joint Custody* Laws In The UNITED STATES , or see ancpr.com/joint_custody_laws_in_ the_united.htm

7 Presumptive Joint Physical Custody Group Report under Minnesota House File 1262 pages 5

LEGAL CHILD CUSTODY

Legal Child Custody is defined as the right to make parental decisions for the child. These include the child's choice of religion, schooling, medical care, diet, discipline, dress, and the like. Like physical child custody, legal child custody can be either granted solely to the Custodial Parent or jointly between both parents.

In the real world, Noncustodial Parents who share "joint *legal* custody" with the Custodial Parent usually have nothing more than an honorary title. This is largely due to the power and influence that Custodial Parents have over children in their custodial households. Custodial Parents and even judges are not very receptive to input coming from the Noncustodial Parent on making parental decisions for the child over the objection of the Custodial Parent unless there are problems at the Custodial Parent's home.

Awarding the Noncustodial parent joint legal custody is kind of like giving crumbs to the loser. It's a prestigious-sounding title with little to no significance or power without the consent of the Custodial Parent. The only main exception is when the parent who was given full physical custody is acting *outrageously* contrary to the best interest of the child. When a parent has "joint legal custody," it is easier to try to correct this type of situation through court action and, if need be, even reopen the issue of which parent should have Physical Child Custody over the child. However, a *contested* change in physical child custody occurs only in extraordinary situations.

RESOLVING CUSTODY AND VISITATION ISSUES

Child custody disputes often turn into a gut-wrenching and hurtful situation for all involved. Greed and vindictiveness often fuel the fire. Because child support significantly increases the standard of living for one of the parents at the other's expense, seeking sole Physical Child Custody can become the key motivating factor on both sides. Parents often fail to cooperatively work together to share joint physical custody out of spite and greed.

When custody or visitation disputes cannot be resolved without litigation, the judge will entertain facts presented by both sides, weigh the facts, and then make a decision based on what the judge feels is in the best interests of the child. There are many things that can influence the judge's decision. Judges often appoint Guardian ad Litems as neutral thirds parties to investigate the facts of the case. Based on their investigations, Guardians make recommendations to the judge.

If the parents can agree on a custody arrangement, judges usually assume that the agreement is in the best interests of the child, unless of course the facts and common sense rebut that assumption.

REBUTTABLE PRESUMPTIONS

There are certain common factual situations deemed so important in resolving the issue of "what is in the best interest of the child" they can legally create *rebuttable presumptions*, which are used to help resolve child custody and visitation issues. Being rebuttable, these presumptions can be rebutted with evidence that challenges the validity of the presumptions.

PRIMARY CARETAKER

The first and often the most important "rebuttable presumption" is to assume it is in the "best interest of the child" to award "physical custody" to the parent who has been the child's "primary caretaker."

The *"primary caretaker"* is the person who has been most responsible for the everyday upbringing and care of the child. In our society this responsibility is often, but not necessarily, assumed by the biological mother. The legal term "primary caretaker" has a different legal meaning than the term "Physical Custodial Parent."

It is not uncommon these days that both parents share the responsibility of being the "primary caretaker," at least to one degree or another, especially if both parents work. Sometimes even the father takes on the main responsibility in raising and caring for the child's physical and emotional needs. It is not all that uncommon that a person other than a biological parent (like a grandparent or a nanny) takes on the responsibility of being a child's primary caretaker.

There's another strong rebuttable presumption that it is in the best interests of the child that biological parents are preferred over all other contenders for child custody. This includes nonparents who have been the child's primary caretaker.

A consensual adoption is the most common way a person who is not a biological parent is awarded to be the Physical Custodial Parent of a child. Two motivators can persuade biological parents to give up their parental rights and responsibilities. First of all, giving away a person's parental rights eliminates the day-to-day responsibility of raising a child. Second, and equally important for some parents, adoption legally eliminates any future child support obligations. The downside is that all legal rights of the parent are given up, including the right to have contact with the child without the consent of the adoptive parent.

There are of course examples of biological parents being stripped of their parental rights to raise and house a child due to gross misdeeds, dangerous incompetence, or abandonment.

Judges are loath to award Physical Child Custody in *contested* cases to someone other than a biological parent. Only if the evidence shows that both biological parents are totally irresponsible due to factors such as a history of chemical dependency, criminal activity, abandonment, or child abuse will a judge even consider awarding Physical Child Custody to someone other than a biological parent without parental consent. Adoption laws vary state by state regarding procedural rules, but for an adoption case to proceed without parental consent, a termination of parental rights hearing will needed.

When determining the best interests of the child, a judge is supposed to, and usually does, give little legal weight to individual parent's rights and feelings. This is true especially in regarding *men* seeking Physical Child Custody. Regardless of some of the improvements in the law regarding physical child custody, keep in mind that women are still highly favored in custody cases—*off the record of course* because it has been established that gender preference in family law is unconstitutional.

Keep in mind the main *legal* reason why women are often preferred in child custody cases. In our society, women are often their children's primary caretakers.

OTHER FACTORS USED TO DETERMINE THE BEST INTERSTS OF THE CHILD

Judges weigh a wide variety of factors other than rebuttable presumptions to determine the best interests of the child. *All the factors used to determine the best interests of the child have one thing in common: they all serve the emotional and physical needs of the child.*

The more relevant a factor is to satisfying the needs of the child, the more legal weight given to that factor. The home environment will be looked at along with the child's preference (especially in regard to older children). A parent's economic status and religion are not given much weight in determining custody issues unless these factors are in some way detrimental to the best interests of the child.

Negative factors are also important considerations—at least as to what is *not* in the best interests of the child. Unstable or dirty home environments are examples. Similarly, child abuse and chemical addiction issues can kill a parent's ability to gain custody. Parents with significant criminal histories and character issues are also highly disfavored.

JOINT PHYSICAL CUSTODY

When a typical divorce occurs, usually only one of the divorcing parents is awarded "Physical Custody" over the child. But that trend has been changing. Both parents are increasingly being awarded "Joint Physical Child Custody." Under a joint physical custody arrangement, both parents are awarded physical custody and are allotted their respective "parenting times" during the calendar year.

JOINT PARENTING TIME

When a joint physical custody arrangement is ordered, the time that the child is ordered to stay with one joint custodial parent or the other is called that parent's *"parenting time."* The judge can order a fifty-fifty split, a twenty-five-seventy-five split, or any other workable time split between the Joint Custodial Parents.

"Parenting time" should not be confused with "visitation time." Visitation only describes the time a child spends "visiting" a Noncustodial Parent. The general rule is that visitation time *does not* reduce a Noncustodial Parent's child support obligations, even if the child has been living with the Noncustodial Parent for a significant period of time! It is not uncommon that the child ends up living with the Noncustodial Parent for a lengthy period of time, even years, with the Custodial Parent's approval. The Noncustodial Parent will still be obligated to pay the Custodial Parent child support *unless and until* the child support order is changed. That's because the general rule is that judges cannot retroactive change past child support obligations which were already ordered in a prior hearing.

The rules regarding child support change dramatically when the parents share Joint Physical Custody over the child. *The percentage of "parenting time" each Joint Custodial Parent is allotted by the judge is directly related to child support obligations, or, should I say, lack thereof.*

The relationship between "parenting time" and calculating child support obligations will be explored in detail in chapter 11. For now, the following hypothetical example will help explain this relationship. If each parent earns exactly the same amount of income per year and were awarded joint physical custody with a fifty-fifty split of "parenting time," neither parent would owe the other any child support. The result would be different if one of the parent earned more than the parent, or if the parenting time was not an exact fifty-fifty split. That's because the parents' relative income to each other along with the percentages of "parenting time" are the main factors used to determine child support obligations when both parents are Joint Custodial Parents.

Joint physical child custody arrangements allow both parents to have meaningful parent-child relationships. The states are becoming increasingly open to joint physical custody arrangements, keeping in mind that allowing a child to have meaningful parent-child relationships with both parents is often in the best interest of the child.

The trend in parenting is changing to where today both parents are increasingly sharing childrearing responsibilities not only during their marriages, and even after they divorce. As mentioned earlier, most states along with the District of Columbia have either rebuttable presumptions or statements of preference that joint custody arrangements are to be in the best interests of the child. However, *the states which have actual presumptions that joint physical custody is in the best interests of the child remains a minority.*[8] It's a long leap in the law from not that long ago, when women were openly preferred to be granted sole physical custody of the parents' children under the largely discredited "tender years doctrine".

VISITATION

"Visitation" is defined as the right of the Noncustodial Parent and child to share time together. Visitation is meant to either continue or establish a parent-child relationship between the Noncustodial parent and the child. *Universally, there is a strong presumption that reasonable visitation between the child and the Noncustodial Parent is in the best interest of the child.* Clear and convincing evidence is needed to rebut this presumption. Unfortunately, under our legal system, the legal right to child visitation for the Noncustodial Parent is often not worth the

---

8 The actual states which have actual rebuttable presumptions favoring joint physical custody remain a minority. "According to the American Bar Association website, several states, including California, Connecticut, Maine, Michigan, Mississippi, Nevada, Tennessee, Vermont, and Washington, adopted laws in favor of joint custody, but only when the parents agreed to it. Other states, including the District of Columbia, Florida, Idaho, Iowa, Kansas, Louisiana, Minnesota, Missouri, Montana, New Hampshire, New Mexico, and Texas, have laws favoring a presumption for joint [physical] custody." Presumptive Joint Physical Custody Group Report under Minnesota House File 1262 page 11.

paper it is written on due to the common mischief of Physical Custodial Parents. Parental alienation incited against the Noncustodial Parent is rampant in this county.

The general rule is that *no credit or reduction in child support* is given to the Noncustodial Parent for visitation.

If the Noncustodial Parent finds himself or herself in the situation of having extended visitation with the child with the consent of the Custodial Parent, the Custodial Parent has the right to motion for Changed Circumstances for a reduction in future support obligations or maybe even joint physical custody with the consent of the other parent. If such a motion is successful, it can change *future* child support obligations, but not those accumulated prior to the motion.

Iowa and some other states have an exception to the general rule that visitation does not reduce the Noncustodial Parent's child support obligations. In these states, Noncustodial Parents are allowed a reduction in child support, *but only if a judge orders that the Noncustodial Parent has an "extended overnight visitation."* The minimum length of Court-ordered "extended overnight visitation" is defined under state law. It usually means over a fourth of the calendar year has been ordered as overnight extended visitation. This appears to me to be a mere appeasement to headstrong women demanding being the sole Physical Custodial Parent, when in reality the parents share joint physical custody together.

Effective enforcement of visitation rights against an adversarial Physical Custodial Parent is all but impossible in the family court environment once an older child has been alienated against the Noncustodial parent. The Noncustodial Parents are often left with the horrible decision of to litigate or give up the battle. If the Custodial Parent unlawfully denies visitation rights to the Noncustodial parent (often defined as a gross-misdemeanor, and also defined as a legitimate ground to file a contempt of court action), the Noncustodial parent still must pay child support to the Custodial Parent or face severe penalties for nonpayment.

There's often a double standard at play regarding the rights of the Custodial parent and Noncustodial parent, and the enforcement of their respective rights. And yes, the Noncustodial parent is often treated like dirt and sanctioned to an involuntary servitude position with the Custodial Parent even when the Custodial Parent is illegally denying visitation rights.

CHAPTER 12

THE OVERLOOKED PLAYERS

Be cautious if any other important players are invited to have their say in your family law case. This may be the case if you have any minor children with your opponent. They can make or break a litigant's chances of prevailing on issues relating to child custody, visitation rights, and child support.

Even if you do have minor children with your opponent, their participation in your case is not guaranteed; it must be triggered by either the judge, differing state laws, or by a request from either party.

GUARDIAN AD LITEMS

A Guardian Ad Litem is appointed by a judge as an advocate to represent the best interests of the child during custody and visitation disputes. They also represent children in child protection cases like those involving child endangerment or abandonment. Some states call Guardians "Court Appointed Special Advocates."

By law, they represent *only* the child's interests, not the parents' interests. Guardians are appointed to act as neutral third parties to investigate a case to help judges determine what is in the best interest of the child. As an advocate for the child, their neutrality on parental interests often disappears because what is in the best interests of the child may be at odds with one or both of the parent's best interests.

After an investigation, Guardians report the facts as they understand them and make recommendations to the judge regarding what they believe is in the best interests of the child. Rather than remaining neutral information gathers, they can become vocal adversaries supporting one or the other parent in the determination of child custody and visitation rights.

Most states protect Guardian ad Litems with "quasi-judicial immunity." This means they can't be sued by a party litigant for their negligence or incompetence. Some states allow Guardians to be sued and defend them with free legal representation and compensate plaintiffs to settle damage claims should they be found negligent. A party litigant can motion to have a Guardian removed "for cause" from a case. But judges are unlikely to be at all sympathetic to such a complainant unless there is found to be a clear personal conflict of interest. Legal attacks against a Guardian should be well grounded and used only as a last resort.

Guardians work as third party fact finders for the judge. They are required to investigate all of the facts of the case relevant to what is in the best interests of the child. This usually includes interviews with each parent, the child, and possibly others. They may inspect residences and living conditions and inquire about parental work commitments. Guardians are usually required to draft written recommendations to the judge regarding "Child Custody" and "Child Visitation" issues. *Judges usually follow and even rubber-stamp Guardian Ad Litems' recommendations into their final court orders.*

Keep in mind that a judge's "legal opinion" can be greatly supported by the Guardian's findings. When a judge drafts an opinion for an order, the judge can write, "A Guardian was appointed to neutrally represent the best interests of the child. The Guardian has made a report to the court including recommendations regarding custody and visitation arrangements. Upon review of the facts and the Guardian's report, the court concurs with the Guardian's recommendations regarding child custody and visitation. Therefore it is hereby ordered that..."

Many states have pathetic educational and professional requirements for their Guardian ad Litems' certification. I found out to my dismay that my state only requires a Guardian to attend a forty-hour classroom course to become certified! That's it! Many states have equally poor certification requirements. Some call them volunteers even when paid for their job.

Luckily, many states require Guardian ad Litems to be licensed attorneys so that they can at least be held accountable under their state attorney ethics board for misconduct. It also helps that they have some idea of the law. It also lessens the real possibility of incompetence and personal bias.

My personal opinion is that Guardian Ad Litems are often prejudiced against men in contested Physical Child Custody cases. My speculation is that it is easier to follow the norm and give women the benefit of the doubt on close child custody issues. It's an unfortunate reality in the family court environment. As a man getting divorced, you have to work a little harder to overcome this type of prejudice. Your starting point is to put on your nice guy hat.

HOW TO DEAL WITH GUARDIAN AD LITEMS

Always keep in mind that if a Guardian becomes involved in your case, the Guardian's first and foremost job is a "finder of fact." In many respects, their job is similar to a jury's job at a trial. A jury's role is also that of a "finder of fact" for the judge. Juries and Guardians both interpret the facts of the case and make factual conclusions.

Guardians are investigators. They listen to facts as presented by both sides, determine the truthfulness of those facts, and weigh them to make a recommendation to the judge on what they believe is in the best interests of the child. But unlike a jury, Guardians often base their opinions on otherwise inadmissible hearsay, personal opinions, biases, and unreliable rumors. Unlike a jury trial, there are no assurances that the information the Guardian uses is credible. This information is relayed to the judge as the basis of the Guardian's findings of fact, which presents an often exploited opportunity for unethical litigants to tip the legal scale in their favor with the judge.

93

Keep in mind the power that Guardians have on resolving child custody and visitation issues. Make a positive impression. Try your best to positively influence the Guardian. Sell yourself on being a good person who is ready, able, and willing to help serve the best interests of the child.

Your second and possibly most important job with the Guardian is to see that the Guardian has an accurate understanding of the facts relating to what is in the best interests of the child. It's a safe bet that your opponent isn't going to present facts that favor your position. That's *your* job. It's also your job to try to rebut any half-truths and lies your opponent may have made to the Guardian. You can ill afford to have the Guardian report false and biased information to the judge.

Party litigants can influence Guardians to favor their own position. Unethical women and men often try to play the Guardian to make recommendations in their favor. Recall that Guardians often rely on otherwise inadmissible and unreliable hearsay to base their recommendations. An often used tactic by women is to falsely portray themselves as being victimized by their male spouse along with their concern that the male spouse may also victimize the children. This topic will be explored in more detail in chapter 16.

Guardians make official recommendations to the judge on which parent should get custody. They also make recommendations regarding visitation schedules. In effect, the Guardian's recommendations set up a rebuttable presumption to the court regarding custody and visitation. Judges, of course, have the power to decide not to follow a Guardian's recommendations. But the chances of a judge acting totally contrary to the Guardian's recommendations are unlikely—extraordinary, for that matter. Think about it. If a judge makes an order directly contrary to the Guardian's recommendations, it could be used as a ground for an appeal by the disenfranchised party litigant.

The best way to deal with Guardian Ad Litems is to positively engage them. Put your nice-guy hat on. A Guardian's first and foremost job is to determine what is in the best interests of the child. That's your opening. Treat the Guardian with respect and act polite. It might take some playacting if the Guardian is a jerk. Guardians are not really meant to be mediators between the party litigants, but they can and do fill that role if they feel it is in the best interests of the child.

Be receptive to any negotiation attempts by the Guardian. It might even help you resolve your issues with your opponent. At a minimum, a sincere effort on your part to resolve issues with your opponent will make you look good in the eyes of the Guardian, which in turn may be relayed to the judge. Listen, instead of speaking too much.

Avoid openly bashing your opponent; it may turn off the Guardian. *Constructive* criticism of your opponent, if overdone under the circumstances, may be seen as bashing. If the Guardian is misled by your opponent, inform the Guardian of the facts supporting your position.

Be reasonable and flexible with the Guardian's suggestions and opinions. You certainly have the right to give your own suggestions and opinions, but do it in a diplomatic way instead of an adversarial way. Try to figure out how to positively influence the Guardian in the determination of what is in the best interests of the child. Your good demeanor and positive, constructive, problem-solving approach will probably get relayed to the judge in the Guardian's report. The same is true if you act like an unreasonable obstructionist or a jerk. Let your opponent make the mistakes with the Guardian, not you.

CHILD SUPPORT OFFICERS

Child Support Officers establish, modify, and enforce child support orders.[9] They work for each state's child support enforcement agency (e.g. Human Services).

---

9 "State Child Support Programs locate noncustodial parents, establish paternity, establish and enforce support orders, modify orders when appropriate, and collect and distribute child support payments. While programs vary from state to state, their services are available to all parents who need them." HANDBOOK ON CHILD SUPPORT ENFORCEMENT, page 1, U.S. Department of Health and Human Services Administration for Children and Families Office of Child Support Enforcement Washington, D.C. 20447

Child Support Officers are powerful child support advocates for Custodial Parents who have either "Permanent" or "Temporary" Physical Custody of a child.

Child Support Officers also are involved in paternity cases, which are used to determine the biological father for child support purposes. Paternity cases are not that uncommon.

When involved in a case, Child Support Officers are *most noted* as being nasty adversarial advocates for Custodial Parents seeking late child support payments from Noncustodial Parents. In instances where the obligor is behind a set number of days in paying child support (which is usually about ninety days), Child Support Officers can motion the court to find the obligor in "Contempt of Court."

When a Noncustodial Parent is found to be in Contempt of Court for failure to make timely child support payments to the Custodial Parent, the judge has an arsenal of nasty sanctions to potentially slap on the Noncustodial Parent. These sanctions include but are not limited to jail sentences, wage garnishments, suspension of driver's licenses, and suspension of professional licenses.

When requested by a party litigant, they can also motion for an increase or decrease in *future* child support payments due to *Changed Circumstances*. Courts will not entertain a motion for changed circumstances unless there has been a "substantial change" in the Parent's income. A substantial change in income often requires that there has been an increase or decrease in the Parents' monthly income to the point that the child support obligation would change by over 20 percent (depending on the jurisdiction). Before a party can request to increase or decrease a child support order, enough time must have elapsed since the last child support order. That amount of time is often three years depending on the jurisdiction.

In their role to establish or modify child support orders, Child Support Officers can motion the judge to "impute" the payer's income to a higher level than the payer is actually earning if they feel the payer is intentionally underemployed. The states are split on allowing judges to impute income.

Child Support Officers are major players in establishing the dollar amount of monthly child support obligations. *When involved in determining the amount of child support payments, the County Child Support Officer will make recommendations to the judge in court regarding his or her opinion as to the dollar amount of the basic monthly child support obligations, along with additional obligations like paying for child medical costs and child daycare costs.* Chapter 12 goes into detail on how child support obligations are determined.

A Custodial Parent going on or applying for welfare assistance automatically triggers the involvement of a child support officer. The reason being is that when a Physical Custodial Parent is drawing welfare, the state becomes the effective "Payee" of the "Payer's" child support obligations. The reason why is to repay the state for the welfare given to the Custodial Parent. Another mandatory trigger is when a Custodial Parent requests assistance in the collection for late child support payments.

When child support payments are not paid on time, the County Child Support Officer often initiates a Contempt of Court action against the payer. The attorney who represents the County Child Support Officer at these hearings is a state *District Attorney.* Yes, this is the same person who prosecutes criminals in criminal court. And yes, an obligor who gets behind in making child support often legitimately feels like a criminal defendant who has already been found guilty and is now awaiting sentencing at a Contempt of Court hearing.

Contempt Hearings often include an Order to Show Cause, where the defendant/respondent is required to prove his or her innocence to prevent nasty court sanctions for failure to make timely child support payments. Orders to Show Cause are attached to Court Summons Orders which order Noncustodial Parents to appear in court to face a Contempt of Court motion. If an obligor fails to personally attend a Contempt of Court hearing, an arrest warrant will likely be ordered. The following is a typical Order to Show Cause notice in a court summons.

"YOU ARE HEREBY ORDERED TO SHOW CAUSE WHY THE COURT
SHOULD NOT FIND YOU IN CONTEMPT OF COURT."

A good analogy for the Child Support Officers in family court is to compare their role to that of a police officer. Both use the District Attorney to prosecute their cases against legal offenders. But unlike criminal law, it is not necessary to prove that there was "intent" to violate a child support order. The issue in these cases is not whether the offender intended to violate a child support order; the issue is whether the offender *did* violate a child support order by not paying child support on time.

Obviously, judges come down even harder on offenders who intentionally violate child support orders than those who are simply unable to pay child support on time. If an obligor *intentionally* fails to make timely child support payment, it can become a criminal matter (possibly a felony).

HOW TO DEAL WITH CHILD SUPPORT OFFICERS

Child Support Officers' main job is to help Custodial Parents to get their child support money. My experience has been that Child Support Officers often don't like dealing much with the payers of child support, and especially not with their attorneys. My guess is that it's because they have learned from their own experiences that many payers despise them, and their attorneys are out to expose their incompetence to the judges.

Child Support Officers are often prejudiced against payers of child support. After all, their main job is to prosecute deadbeat parents. It's also because they often only have a one-sided version of the story coming from the Custodial Parent and his or her attorney. This can and does lead to unnecessary and sometimes unjust motions to impute an obligor's income.

If you are likely to end up an obligor, deal with the Child Support Officers from Human Services in a businesslike manner when they request information from you. Like any discovery requests from an opponent, seek legal advice from your attorney on how to proceed. If you think the way to deal with them is to cuss and yell at them, you will probably make them trigger happy against you. You don't want them to make a recommendation out of personal spite, like asking the judge to impute your income to a higher level than you are actually earning.

DISTRICT ATTORNEYS

District Attorneys play a key role advocating for County Child Support Officers. When a County Child Support Officer makes recommendations to find an Obligor of child support in Contempt of Court for failure to make timely child support payments, the local state District Attorney acts as the prosecutor at the motion hearing.

The District Attorney is the acting attorney for the state handling a variety of family law matters, including CHIP (child in need of protection) cases. Most of the cases that the District Attorney prosecutes in family court are against obligors who fail to make timely child support payments.

These type of hearing are actually civil court actions. Because they are civil court actions, payers of child support are not given the same procedural protections as criminals are given in criminal court. Be aware that penalties for civil Contempt of Court can be severe, including possible revocation of driving privileges and jail time. That doesn't sound all that "civil" to me. I label it *quasi-criminal* prosecutions.

A disproportionate number of people in family court also end up in criminal court defending themselves for host of crimes, including violations of Protection Orders, Domestic Abuse, Child Endangerment, intentional evasion of child support obligations, and similar criminal offenses. All criminal prosecutions are handled and prosecuted by the county's District Attorney Office.

A good piece of advice is to never talk to a police officer, the opposing attorney, or a District Attorney while you have a divorce pending! This is an example of when you should "just keep your trap shut" (Chapter 15). If you have an attorney, District Attorneys and any opposing attorneys for that matter, cannot talk to you directly. Attorneys are prohibited under each state's Attorney Ethics Rules from talking to opposing attorneys' clients.

Police can question you *unless* you tell them you do not to talk to them. Expect them to try to trick you (even lie to you) to get you to answer questions even after you say you refuse to answer any questions. If you tell them you want an attorney to represent you, police are prohibited from asking you any interrogating questions after that point.

CHAPTER 13

CHILD CUSTODY AND VISITATION STREET SMARTS

The last two chapters covered the basics on how child custody and visitation issues are determined. They are both determined by answering a simple question: *what is in the "best interest of the child?"*

This chapter focuses on how that question is resolved by the judge within the family court environment. The approach you use to resolve your family law issues can drastically influence the outcome of those issues. How much so depends largely on the cards you've already been dealt along with how both you and your opponent play your cards. Expect new cards, opportunities, and minefields to be dealt during the process.

You learned that Guardian ad Litems (i.e. Court Appointed Special Advocates) often become involved to represent the best interests of the child when there are custody and visitation issues. They are appointed by judges to do impartial fact finding to advocate for the best interests of the child. They make recommendations to the judge on custody and visitation issues. Judges usually (but not always) follow their recommendations. You learned the best way of dealing with Guardians is by using the nice-guy approach and showing yourself to be devoted to serving the best interests of the child.

THE JUDGE'S THOUGHT PROCESS

When litigating family law issues before a judge, it's important to focus on how the judge's thinking will likely resolve those issues. A good attorney will try to present a legal argument that is in sync with a judge's thought process, predispositions, and even personality based on prior dealings with the judge.

It is important to remember that a judge's job is to resolve legal issues on a mass scale in a legal system properly termed an *adversarial court system*. By necessity, judges have to rely heavily on negotiated settlements in both criminal and civil court settings. Regardless of whether the case is resolved with a settlement or through litigation, the judge must see to it that the issues are resolved fairly between the adversarial parties using applicable state law as applied to the facts of the case.

Obviously, when resolving child custody issues, judges have to determine what is in the best interests of the child, not what is in the best interests of the parents. When a judge makes an order resolving a family law issue, the judge has to present a logical reason for the decision in writing. This is called the judge's *written opinion*. Judges attach their written opinions to their court orders. A judge's written opinion will state the important relevant facts of the case that swayed the judge in making his or her decision along with applicable state law.

When rationalizing the outcome of custody issues, judges often rely on rebuttable presumptions. Recall that rebuttable presumptions arise from key facts of the case that are commonly used to resolve custody and visitation issues. The easiest and most logical way for a judge to start a legal analysis is to review the facts to determine whether they form rebuttable presumptions. Attorneys use the same approach to advocate their client's case to the judge.

If you have a custody or visitation dispute, provide the judge and your opponent, for negotiation purposes, with the facts that show why it is in the best interests of the child that your position should prevail. Like a good politician, you and your attorney should nail the important facts without losing your audience in the details or on irrelevant matters. Target your audience like a marksman to anyone you have to inform or persuade in the family law environment, including your own attorney.

Objectively listen to the other side's version of the story. It can help you get a good idea of the cards that are on the table. Read the judge. Judges are not shy about telling the parties what they are thinking, either expressly or through nonverbal body language. Judges can be swayed with common sense approaches to resolve family law issues. Conflicting rebuttable presumptions may even arise. For instance, the rebuttable presumption favoring the Primary Caretaker often conflicts with the rebuttable presumption that Joint Physical Custody is in the best interests of the child.

Before exploring this area of law in more depth, a short review is in order regarding the rebuttable presumptions judges use to determine "what is in the best interests of the child."

First of all, biological parents are preferred to have Physical Child Custody over all others who are not the child's biological parent. This preference overrides even nonparent Primary Caretakers.

The child's Primary Caretaker is the person who has been most involved with the care and upbringing of the child. A biological parent who has been the primary caretaker over a child is generally preferred over all others. This preference does not necessarily preclude the other parent from being awarded the Physical Custodial Parent or from being awarded a Joint Custodial Parent, especially if both parents acted as the Primary Caretaker to some degree or another.

The states are increasingly receptive to the notion that children do best when the parents share joint physical child custody. *An increasing minority of states have rebuttable presumptions which presume that joint custody is in the best interests of the child.*[10] It's a bold recognition that it is in the best interests of the child to receive love and emotional support from both parents.

---

10 http://archive.leg.state.mn.us/docs/2009/mandated/090065.pdf Presumption Study Group Report, page 10, January 14, 2009

There is also a strong rebuttable presumption that "reasonable visitation" with the Noncustodial Parent is in the best interests of the child. The definition of "reasonable visitation" depends on the factual circumstances of the case together with what the judge believes is in the best interests of the child. Visitation issues do not usually hinge on whether the Noncustodial Parent *should* be allowed reasonable visitation. The main issue instead is defining what is "reasonable" under the circumstances.

A judge's order for "supervised visitation," meaning that a social worker or other responsible third party must be present during visitation, or that visitation must be held at police headquarters, may be reasonable in certain extreme circumstances where there is evidence of child endangerment, but outlandishly unreasonable in almost all other circumstances.

A typical "reasonable" visitation order in most cases allows the child to have overnight visitation with the Noncustodial Parent every other weekend, along with every other holiday rotating yearly. Weeklong vacations are often also included.

Plain old common sense dictates that it is in the best interest of the child when the parents can make an agreement regarding child custody and visitation issues. Judges prefer settlement agreements regarding these issues and often pressure the divorcing couple's attorneys to pressure their clients to come up with one. Parents able to peacefully negotiate these issues gain the peace of mind that they will be insured against any wild cards thrown at them due to the judge's use of discretion. It's also in everyone's best interests to try to avoid an ugly custody or visitation battle.

DEVELOP INFORMED STRATEGIES

Neutrally review the facts of your case. Who's been the Primary Caretaker? Chances are good that you both have been in some way or other. Are you and your opponent willing to come up with a reasonable custody or visitation arrangement? What are the facts in your case that are most relevant to resolving what is in the best interests of the child? Facts that positively foster the child's emotional and physical development along with the child's general well-being are given the most weight in determining what is in the best interests of the child. Is there a presumption or statement of preference in your state which states that joint physical custody is in the best interests of the child?

By now, you should be getting a good insight into the family law environment and know what the relevant facts are in your case. A simple analysis of your circumstances should give you a good idea of the cards that both you and your opponent hold. With logic as a guide, you should have a good idea of the likely outcome of your family law issues should your case turn into a custody battle. Remember, she has one card you don't. She is a woman. Although judges deny it, gender discrimination still strongly influences the outcome in Child Custody cases.

When it comes to the highly emotional issue of child custody, don't provoke a custody battle with a baseless poker bluff with a determined adversary who has cards clearly better than your own. This type of strategy will not only piss off your opponent, it will piss off the judge and all the other important players who may become involved in your case. An all-out declaration of war based on a poker bluff that has been called, usually leads to expensive, needless, and painful litigation. It will also *lessen* your chances of a favorable outcome regarding your custody or visitation issues.

One of the best cards you could be dealt is an opponent who is willing to be reasonable and flexible regarding child custody and visitation. Although it may be difficult to impossible to bring out the better side of your opponent when going through a divorce with her, act reasonable, flexible, and noble. You can catch flies with honey but not with vinegar, as the old saying goes. If your soon-to-be ex responds to your gentlemanly behavior by acting like a bat out of hell, your positive and noble approach will likely help sway the judge and the other important players involved in your case. Let her be the bad guy.

Some women are open to the option to negotiate a Joint Physical Custody arrangement, unless provoked or pissed off. Point out that a joint custody arrangement would give her more free time to do her own thing without the constant sole responsibility and burden of childrearing.

Some women are actually more interested in the best interest of the children than padding their bank account with child support. There are also some women who are simply unable or unwilling to be responsible for the upbringing of a child.

Unfortunately greed and power fuel many child custody battles. Many women have the mind-set that children are their property, which can and should be used to extract as much financial gain as possible from their former spouse. Similarly, there are some selfish men who choose a custody battle solely for selfish and vindictive purposes with little or no regard for what is in the best interest of the child.

What is perhaps the most disturbing are the redneck hotheads on both sides who simply want to make a pointless point out of anger. "I'm right and you're wrong, and the hell with you. I'm going to show the world that you're a loser in court, loser!"

TEMPORARY CUSTODY LEADS TO PERMANENT CUSTODY

As far as custody strategies go, first obtaining temporary physical custody over a child as a means to obtain permanent sole physical custody is the method of choice to win custody battles. Why? Because it usually works.

This is a strategy that you want to look out for, or even possibly use yourself. It is based on the following simple fact in family court: *if a litigant is successful motioning for "temporary physical custody" over a child during the divorce proceedings, it usually leads to "Permanent Physical Custody" in the final divorce decree.*

There's an old legal saying that still holds very true today regarding legal ownership rights. You may have heard it. It simply states that "possession is nine-tenths of the law."

So what is "temporary custody" over a child, and how does one obtain it? Temporary custody over a child is the result of a judge ordering that one of the parents has "Temporary Sole Physical Custody" over a child until the parties and the court have time to address the issue of Permanent Physical Custody. The legal theory is that a short motion hearing is adequate "due process" to address the issue of temporary child custody during the early court proceedings. When the parties and the court are able to fully address the issue of permanent physical custody later in the court proceedings, full due process will be then offered to both parents.

There's one big problem with that theory. Temporary Physical Custody almost always leads to Permanent Physical Custody because the parent who was awarded Temporary Physical Custody becomes the acting Primary Caretaker of the child. Primary Caretakers have the benefit of the Primary Custodial presumption over the other parent. On top of that, a change in status of the Temporary Physical Custodial Parent along with a change in residence will be seen as emotionally disturbing to the child.

When a judge tells the litigants at a temporary custody hearing that temporary custody will not make an impact on the final decision regarding permanent physical custody, he or she is lying. Besides the Primary Caretaker presumption, which is used to determine the Physical Custodial Parent, judges are reluctant to change the status quo of where the child is living, once it has already been legally established. Anything that disrupts the child's emotional state is deemed to be not in the best interest of the child. This includes reversing the status quo of the parents by reversing which parent is acting as the Primary Caretaker and acting as Physical Custodial Parent. If there is a change in the status quo regarding physical child custody, the aggrieved litigant will scream that her parental rights have been stripped for no legal reason. This might even raise another rebuttable presumption that changing child custody is not in the best interests of the child without clear and convincing evidence showing why it is necessary.

If both litigants have similar chances of obtaining physical custody through litigation, a strategy some women are willing to resort to in order to win Permanent Physical Custody is to obtain a Protection Order against the husband. Assuming the Protection Order is approved, which they usually are because it is hard to prove one's innocence once assumed guilty in an Ex Parte proceeding, the person benefiting from the protection order usually will be given Temporary Physical Custody over the couple's children. It doesn't take a rocket scientist to guess who will be given sole Permanent Physical Custody over the children in that situation. Many states have strong rebuttable presumptions that if there is evidence of domestic abuse, it is not in the best interests of the child to allow the abuser to have physical child custody.[11]

JOINT PHYSICAL CUSTODY

If one of your realistic goals is to obtain Physical Child Custody, and your cards aren't that great compared to hers, consider requesting Joint Physical Custody. Joint Physical Custody is an arrangement where both parents are granted joint physical custody of the child according to a percentage of Parenting Time during each calendar year. Unlike most visitation arrangements, a joint custody arrangement at least allows each parent the chance to have a *true* parent-child relationship. But carefully consider the option before jumping in. The rewards have to outweigh the drawbacks. You also have to have the proper cards in order to play this hand. Remember, more than half of all states have either rebuttable presumptions or statements of preference that it is in the best interests of the child that parents share Joint Physical Custody. In the other states, it is fair game to try to persuade the judge and your opponent that it is in the best interests of the child to share custody.

Obviously, there can be a lot of drawbacks that accompany the responsibility of being a Joint Custodial Parent. The likely drawbacks and other obstacles should be carefully considered before making a commitment. These problems range from having to deal with simple

---

11 "Twenty-two States have presumptions against joint custody where there is a history of domestic violence, child abuse, sexual abuse, and/or where a parent has been convicted of certain crimes." Presumption Study Group Report, http://archive.leg.state.mn.us/docs/2009/mandated/090065.pdf

logistical problems all the way to having to deal with serious personality conflicts with your opponent, and maybe even with your own child.

In order to make a joint custody arrangement work, the parents have to work together. At a minimum, they have to work out logistical problems and avoid the temptation to badmouth the other parent. If future problems arise with one or both of the parents' conduct, the judge will not be happy with the person or persons responsible.

If both parents agree to a joint physical custody arrangement in a Settlement Agreement, judges are usually receptive to the proposal. But the arrangement has to make sense. The judge will require a workable plan be provided in writing. Such a plan makes good sense because it lets everyone involved to be fully aware of the rules of conduct and procedure.

A sensible arrangement in a settlement agreement might agree upon sharing physical custody during different parts of the calendar year or during different periods of the development of the child. Keep in mind, however, it is unlikely a judge would allow a joint physical custody arrangement if the parents are constantly at each other's throats. The judge will not be the referee between two battling spouses. Judges can and sometimes do punish troublemakers who mess up joint custody arrangements. It's unlikely, but a judge may even entertain a change in custody.

Under most circumstances, requesting Joint Physical Custody is a reasonable claim if the person requesting it is able, ready, and willing to take on the responsibility. An added benefit for making a Joint Physical Custody request is that it might convince the judge and your opponent that you are truly concerned for what is in the best interests of the child by being willing to work together with your opponent. If sole physical custody is not in the cards, joint physical custody is an avenue to have a meaningful relationship with your child. It would also reduce or eliminate the burden of huge monthly child support payments.

Such an arrangement necessitates cooperation from both parents. Even if a reasonable Joint Physical Custody request is ruled out by the judge, it might make the judge more compassionate and receptive toward you when resolving other issues, including reasonable visitation. It can even help with a potential change in custody in the future if there is a "dramatic change in circumstances" with the Custodial Parent's ability to raise the child.

Many states, and judges in the states that don't, *require* that the joint custodial parents enter into a *Parenting Plan*. These are often called "Parenting Agreements." Regardless if it is required or not, it just makes common sense for both parties to have a court-ordered, flexible Parenting Agreement. Such a plan can help keep both sides in line and helps prevent problems down the road. It also discourages selective memory problems.

A major consideration the judge will look at to determine whether joint physical custody is practical is to determine whether each parent is able and committed to devote a substantial amount of time to the care and upbringing of the child. Each parent must be able to provide an adequate home and social environment. Schooling and logistical considerations must also be addressed along with anything else important to the best interests of the child.

The starting point to achieve joint physical custody of your child is to come off as a likeable parent who just happened to find himself in divorce court.

REQUEST TO CHANGE CHILD'S LAST NAME

Sometimes a woman will petition or motion the judge to change the child's last name from the father's to the mother's maiden name or newly acquired remarried last name. This is usually a vile attempt to alienate the child from the Noncustodial Parent and inflict emotional harm. These petitions are usually motivated out of spite and personal selfishness. Thankfully, the law and the courts frown on them. Judges are usually unwilling to grant these motions over protest of the Noncustodial father. The legal hurdle the Custodial mother has to jump over is to prove that a name a name change *is necessary to prevent undue hardship* on the child. This, as a high legal standard, makes it *all but impossible* to change the minor child's last name over objections of the other parent unless the parent is infamous and people would frown on the child because of the association with the infamous parent.

CUSTODY CHANGES

Understandably, judges are very reluctant to order a change of physical custody over a child. It can be accomplished in a motion hearing. Judges use a very high standard of proof when considering ordering a change in physical child custody. Child endangerment and abandonment allegations are the types of substantial changes in circumstances necessary for a judge to even seriously consider a motion for a custody change. Once again, the best interest of the child standard is used to determine the outcome.

In conclusion, advocate your position reasonably without be pretentious. Don't pick fights when you don't have a reasonable chance of winning. This should not be confused with caving in on your rights! Stand up for your rights in a smart way. What I am saying is *think* before you act.

The good news is that judges are quite susceptible to approving parental agreements regarding Physical Child Custody and Visitation. It is in your best interests to try to come up with a fair and reasonable agreement on these issues. The potential long-term gain of acting in good faith far exceeds the very *likely* risk of being put down by a vindictive opponent. But even if your opponent acts like a vindictive jerk, you can handle it. And guess who is going to look better in the eyes of the important parties that are involved in the case? You! Guess who is going to look back on this ordeal with minimal personal regrets? You!

CHAPTER 14

CHILD SUPPORT

The birth of a child creates legal obligations upon the biological parents for the child's care and upbringing. This obligation applies regardless whether the biological parents were ever married or not. The legal obligations of parents along with all legal rights and privileges associated with parenting can be transferred from a biological parent to an adoptive parent. When a judge orders that one of the parents is the Physical Custodial Parent over a child, the Noncustodial Parent becomes legally obligated to pay child support to the Custodial Parent until the child reaches the "age of majority."

Basic Child Support is the legal term used to describe the basic monthly financial obligation that a judge orders a Noncustodial parent to pay to the Custodial Parent. *Basic child support obligations are determined primarily, but not exclusively, by ordering a percentage of the Noncustodial monthly income to be paid to the Custodial Parent.* There are several *other* factors also used when calculating Noncustodial Parents' basic child support obligations.

In addition to basic child support payments, the Noncustodial Parent might end up paying a prorated share, a lesser share, or even all of the child's *Child Medical Costs* and *Child Daycare Costs*. If a child support order includes Child Medical Costs and Child Daycare Costs, then the total monthly child support obligation is explained in the following equation:

Total monthly child support obligation = basic child support + (child medical and child daycare costs)

Child medical costs include purchasing medical, vision, and dental insurance along with any out-of-pocket child medical expenses not covered by insurance. Child Daycare Costs are the costs *incurred by the Custodial Parent for employment purposes.*

CHILD MEDICAL COSTS

Child Medical Costs and Child Daycare Cost are usually, *but not necessarily,* divided between both the Noncustodial Parent and the Custodial Parent based on each parent's relative income compared to the couple's combined income. For instance, if one parent earns twice as much as the other, the higher-earning parent often will be ordered to pay twice as much toward child medical costs than the other parent. But then again, judges have the discretion to order one parent to pay a greater share. Your state may have recommendations in its Statutory Child Support Guidelines on how to calculate the parent's recommended share of these expenses. Payment for Child Medical Expenses may be a factor in the state's Child Support Guidelines for reducing the Noncustodial Parent's "basic" child support obligation.

Judges encourage a reduction of these extra, related expenses by the use of either of the parents' employment medical and daycare plans.

CHILD DAYCARE COSTS

Court-ordered *Child Daycare Costs are to be used only for the purpose of allowing the Custodial Parent to work—period.* They are not intended to be used to cover simple babysitting costs. Some states actually require by statute that the Noncustodial Parent help pay for the *Child Daycare Costs.* In other states, it is up to the judge's discretionary powers to order the Noncustodial Parent to pay for them and if so, how much. In either case, judges should (but some don't) specify the conditions and up to what age Child Daycare obligations terminate. Noncustodial Parents ordered to pay for Child Daycare Costs should seek some form of accountability in the judge's order to help ensure that the money is actually spent on Child Daycare Costs and for how long the obligation lasts. It shouldn't last past the child's thirteenth birthday unless the child is handicapped and the judge so orders. Most teenagers simply don't need babysitting to allow the custodial parent to work.

Child Daycare costs are often confusingly called "Child Care Costs" in some jurisdictions. Similarly, alimony is often called "spousal maintenance" or "spousal care" in some jurisdictions. Perhaps the reason for the choice in terms is to make it more palatable for obligors to digest, albeit at the expense of clarity.

CHILD SUPPORT ENDS AT AGE OF MAJORITY

When a child reaches the "age of majority," the Noncustodial Parent's monthly child support obligation terminates. The age of majority is similar to but not exactly the same as legal adulthood, at least when it pertains to the age a young person is allowed to serve in the military or legally drink.

The states vary somewhat on when a child reaches the age of majority in their state. Many states define the age of majority as when a child reaches eighteen years old, others say nineteen years old, and still others say twenty-one years old. Many states have laws that allow judges to extend child support past the age of majority until a child completes high school or completes college. States also give judges the discretion to extend child support past the age of majority for handicapped children.

Support payments can be shorted for a child who has legally been found to be "emancipated" from the household. A child can be declared to be emancipated for child support purposes when a child becomes legally married, joins the military, or is living independently as a self-sustaining adult outside of the Custodial Parent's household.

STATE STATUTORY CHILD SUPPORT GUIDELINES

Every state uses its own state Statutory Child Support Guidelines to calculate the state's recommended child support obligations. State child support guidelines differ somewhat from state to state, but each calculate recommended child support obligations according to key differing factors involved in each case. Judges are not strictly bound to follow their state's "recommended" child support obligations. They have the power to deviate from the state's recommended child support calculations if convinced a departure would be more appropriate and fair under the individual circumstances of a case. Still, judges usually follow the state's recommended child support calculations closely.

The factors used by child support guidelines are specific to the facts each case. For example, an obligor ordered to pay child support for two children is obviously going to end up having to pay more total child support than for just one child. Similarly, Noncustodial Parents with higher incomes will be ordered to pay more child support for their children than lower income Noncustodial Parents. Child support obligations are primarily based on Noncustodial Parents' monthly income.

DISCRETIONARY POWER TO DEVIATE

When judges deviate from the recommended child support obligations, the overall consideration is what is in the best interests of the child. Unmanageable child support obligations lead to defaults which lead to severe legal problems for Noncustodial Parents which in turn can reduce their ability to pay *any* child support. Trying to get blood out of a turnip is obviously not in the best interests of the child. Conversely, a higher standard of living for the child is in the best interests of the child if the Noncustodial Parent has sufficient means to pay for it.

It is fair game for both the Noncustodial Parent and the Custodial Parent to make a "fairness argument" regarding financial hardship. The main argument is that the state's recommended child support obligation is not fair under the circumstances of the case. A financial hardship claim sometimes uses factors that *other states* use, but which aren't used in the local state's child support guidelines.

Keep in mind that Child Support Officers often become involved in helping judges to establish monthly child support obligations. If a Child

Support Officer becomes involved in your case, you want to make sure the officer is aware of the factors that favor your position, and is not mislead by your opponent regarding your financial circumstances. If a Child Support Officer does become involved in a case, it is important to know that they can and sometimes do motion the judge to deviate from the recommended child support obligations. When a deviation is motioned for, it is a safe bet that it is going to be against the Noncustodial Parent.

When involved in cases where no prior child support orders have been issued, Child Support Officers often make initial recommendations on establishing the monthly child support obligations. They do so by gathering the financial facts of a case. Using that information, they sometimes estimate the incomes of the parties. Using the information they gathered or estimated, they then calculate the monthly child support obligation using the state's Child Support Guidelines. They often seek to recover child support retroactively to the date of the separation or the filing of the divorce suit assuming no prior child support orders were issued in a case. Many Noncustodial Parents find themselves immediately seriously behind in their child support payments the first day the initial child support order is issued.

When an issue arises on whether the judge should deviate from the child support guidelines, Child Support Officers are often key players. They typically advocate for Custodial Parents, but there are rare exceptions. If a Child Support Officer suspects that a Noncustodial Parent is intentionally unemployesd or underemployed, the officer may recommend that the judge to impute the Noncustodial Parent's income to a higher income level in order to increase the monthly child support obligation to a level that the judge feels the Noncustodial Parent could be earning.

When using a "fairness argument," it is important to be informed of rationales that can be used as arguments to deviate from your state's recommended child support obligation. The following few paragraphs in this subsection are examples of "fairness arguments" which can be used to try to persuade a judge to deviate from the state's recommended child support obligation:

A *majority of states* use the Physical Custodial Parent's income as a factor *in an addition* to the Noncustodial Parent's income when determining child support obligations. Maybe it is unfair in your case that the *Custodial Parent's income* isn't being used as a factor to set basic child support like the majority of states require. Maybe the Noncustodial Parent's past income is an unfair representation of current income due to a recent reduction in hours, a recent injury, or a recent lay-off.

Conversely, maybe the Noncustodial Parent just got a large promotion and should pay more child support than past income tax records suggest. Maybe the Noncustodial Parent is rich and either is retired or intentionally underemployed. Maybe the Noncustodial Parent is self-employed and his or her actual disposable income isn't in sync with reportable tax income due to tax loop holes. Maybe someone is a tax dodger and lying regarding his or her true reportable taxable income.

The states are split on whether to calculate child support on the payer's before-tax income or after-tax income. Maybe it is unfair in your case that your state calculates child support based on before-tax income rather than after-tax income. Maybe the Noncustodial parent has unusually high commuting expenses which are not deductible. Maybe it would be fairer under the circumstances to allow the Noncustodial Parent to receive the Dependent Child Deduction along with an accompanying Child Tax Credit instead of having it go automatically to the Custodial Parent by legal default under the tax code. *As you can see, additional factors which aren't included in a state's Child Support Guidelines can be used to try to influence a judge to deviate from the state's recommended child support obligations.*

PRIOR CHILD SUPPORT AND ALIMONY OBLIGATIONS

Prior, ongoing child support and alimony obligations are factors that reduce subsequent child support obligations. However, *subsequent support obligations generally do not reduce prior child support obligations.* First in time is first in line.

Prior existing child support and alimony obligations do not reduce subsequent child support obligations dollar for dollar like a tax credit would. Instead, they are used in the child support calculations to reduce the obligor's monthly income for calculating child support. Income after all is *the key factor* used to calculate child support obligations. Factoring in prior support obligations ends up only fractionally reducing later child support obligations (like regular tax deductions only fractionally reduce income tax obligations).

A Noncustodial Parent may have *other* dependent biological children he is providing for who *are not* covered under any other prior child support order. For instance, a Noncustodial Parent might be the biological parent of another child from a different relationship. The child may be living with this parent and being provided for. If so, the support given to this 'other' dependent child should be factored into any subsequent child support order.

DETERMINE THE "RECOMMENDED" CHILD SUPPORT OBLIGATION IN YOUR CASE

If you have any minor children with your opponent, become familiar with *your* state's Statutory Child Support Guidelines and *all the factors* your state uses in the calculation.

The Guidelines differ from state to state regarding the formulas they use, and the relevancy of the *'factors'* and formulas they use to calculate the Non-Custodial parents' recommended monthly child support obligations.

With that said, each state's Statutory Child Support Calculators are far more similar than dissimilar. However, some of the states' recommended child support obligations are arguably less fair and callus to the basic financial needs of Non-Custodial parents than others. This is particularly true with low income working people who often end up with unmanageable child support obligations.

Keep in mind that state Statutory Child Support Guidelines are continuously changing and updating to reflect new on-going changes in the law. Fortunately, many of the current ongoing changes are attempts to make the law less draconian against the truly dead-broke (as opposed to the deadbeat) Non-Custodial Parents.

STATE ONLINE CHILD SUPPORT CALCULATORS

The easiest way to determine the *recommended* child support obligation in your own case is to use your state's online Child Support Calculator. Online Child Support Calculators are relatively easy to use even for a computer novice. They are also updated to be current to reflect any recent changes in the law. They give litigants a good idea where they stand on child support obligations.

Each state has its own online Child Support Calculator website. They use simple fill-in-the-blank questions directly related to the factors that state uses to calculate its recommended child support obligations.

A side note: These websites are often sponsored by each state's Department of Human Services (the same folks who often recommend future child support obligations to the judge and enforce prior delinquent child support obligations against Noncustodial parents). I have no idea if the data from these sites are recorded or not. Giving out personal information is not necessary on these state websites (even when they ask for it). There certainly isn't anything wrong with using John Doe and a nonexistent court file number for your own research purposes if the site asks for your name and court file number.

If you have any minor children related to the divorce proceeding, it's a good idea to have an estimate of about how much you will either have to pay or will be paid to you before the judge orders it. You may want to request a deviation from the state recommended child support obligation.

Noncustodial Parents should keep in mind that an unusual spike in income just prior to the child support hearing should be made known to the judge and opposing side if that spike doesn't fairly represent their true income. Unusual overtime, one-time bonuses, and other unusual upward bumps in income shouldn't carry too much weight in determining the Noncustodial Parent's average monthly income.

If you want to look at the written law itself, your state's Statutory Child Support Guidelines can be found in your state's statutes or online.

Most county courthouses have legal libraries open to the public where you can look up your state statutes either in books or online.

The best and easiest way to understand your state's calculation of its recommended child support obligations is to review and actually use your state's online Child Support Calculator.

IMPUTED INCOME

Many states openly allow judges the power to "impute" a Noncustodial Parent's income to a higher level than he or she is actually earning. The rationale is that some Noncustodial Parents will intentionally earn less income with the sole intent to lower child support obligations. Teary-eyed, bawling Custodial Parents often cry, "Impute the deadbeat's income!" as a tactic to obtain larger child support awards.

Even in states that do not officially allow judges the power to impute the payer's income, judges still have the power to deviate from the state's recommended child support obligations. An allegation that the payer is intentionally under-earning certainly might influence a judge.

The typical game regarding child support is that the Custodial Parent often tries to make the Noncustodial Parent's income look as high as possible in order to obtain higher child support. They sometimes allege that their soon-to-be ex is making money on the side and underreporting income. They typically allege the payer is lazy and unwilling to fulfill their legal obligations to their children. They are quick to point out recent inheritances even though gifts of any sort are not reportable income for the Statutory Child Support Guidelines.

Noncustodial Parents on the other hand often adopt strategies to make their income look as low as possible, especially if they are self-employed and have the ability to use creative tax accounting; some do actually underreport income.

Many litigants don't realize that imputing the Noncustodial 's income is a double-edged sword in that it can also be used to impute the income of the Custodial Parent as well. Yes, Custodial Parent's income can also be imputed if the judge feels the Custodial Parent is intentionally being underemployed or not reporting taxable income. That's because most states use the Custodial Parent's income in addition to the Noncustodial Parent's as an additional factor in determining the state's basic recommended child support obligations. Even in states that don't even consider the Custodial Parent's income in determining basic child support, many states and individual judges proportionally divide Child Medical Costs and Child Daycare Costs according the proportion of the Noncustodial Parent's to the parents' combined income.

Yes, there are those willing to kick themselves in the face by having to survive on a miserably low income in order to pay less to a former spouse. It's a bitter pill to swallow forking out money to increase an ex's standard of living at the expense of your own standard of living. But regardless of those who are bitter and intentionally earning less income with the hope of having a reduced child support obligation, the imputed income net is large and catches many in its path.

Unfortunately, imputing income can and does catch those who were simply trying their best to make ends meet before a divorce, leaving them destitute and having to live their lives in poverty and involuntary servitude for years on end after a support order. Such is the plight of the low-income working class. It's been that way since the beginning of civilization.

POVERTY STATUS

Legitimate welfare or public assistance payments to the Noncustodial Parent can temporarily limit (but not usually eliminate) parents child support obligations to the state's standard minimum obligation due. An obvious attack on any hardship claim is that the obligor is intentionally out of work or is lazy and the judge should impute the obligor's income level to what the obligor could and should be earning.

Also, if the obligor is serving a significant jail sentence, the obligor can motion to reduce child support obligations to the state minimum until released. Even if successful, the child support obligations may keep adding up as delinquent child support obligations (called *arrears*). There are individual state laws that allow obligors to motion for a temporary suspension child support obligations for inmates with lengthy jail sentences, for instance, for those in jail eighteen months or longer.

MONTHLY INCOME

The Noncustodial Parent's monthly income is by far the most important factor in determining child support obligations. Income for child support calculations includes any reportable income for income tax purposes.

One of the biggest issues in determining child support obligations is to determine what income level should be used to compute the obligor's child support obligation. This issue is relatively easy to answer in the case of a long-time employee with a steady income. Other cases are not that easy, and the income level used in the determination of child support should be estimated as fairly as possible. In this type of situation, it is a fair argument on either side that it should higher or lower.

To estimate the obligor's income for child support purposes, all reportable income must be included. In addition to regular forms of income, include additional "benefit" incomes being received by *either* parent, including unemployment income, Social Security retirement income, pension income, and any disability income (including Social Security Disability Income, SSDI). Not only are these extra forms of income for child support purposes, they can also be garnished for child support just like regular wages. Supplemental Security Income, SSI, is an exception to this rule because it is considered subsistence welfare instead of income.

As mentioned in the last subsection, one time gifts and inheritances are not considered income under the Statutory Child Support Guidelines. However, the *income* that they generate is considered income for child support purposes. When judges consider deviating from the state's

123

recommended child support calculations, a sizable inheritance or gift might be considered as one of the factors in justifying a deviation. The minority view in some jurisdictions see regular gifts given over a long period of time, like those from an annuity, are income usable for child support calculations.

Under the Court Rules of Civil Procedure, each side can use the various "Discovery" methods to access financial information from the opposing side. By law, a party to a divorce suit must release this information to the other side *if requested* or face court sanctions for failure to comply with discovery requests. Discovery requests are explained in more detail in chapter 16.

TWO DIFFERENT APPROACHES IN STATE CHILD SUPPORT GUIDELINES

The biggest and perhaps most important difference among the states' Child Support Guidelines is whether the state includes the Custodial Parent's income into the calculations in addition to the Noncustodial Parent's income. The trend (now majority) is to include the Custodial Parent's income as an additional factor into the child support calculations (along with the Noncustodial Parent's income).

INCOME SHARES METHOD

Most states use what is called the *Income Shares Model* when calculating child support obligations. Rather than *only* factoring in the Noncustodial Parent's income to calculate child support, *both parents combined income is used in the calculation.*

Under this method, the Noncustodial Parent's monthly obligation is calculated on what percentage the Noncustodial Parent's income is compared to the combined total income of both parents. Then, the Custodial Parent is given a monthly credit for caring for the child. Due to the credit given to the Custodial Parent for raising the child, the Noncustodial Parent always ends up paying the Custodial Parent child support even when the Noncustodial Parents are earn significantly less.

The states that use both parents' income to calculate the Noncustodial Parent's child support obligation can reduce the Noncustodial Parent's child support obligation, but often not as much as a person would expect regarding basic child support, unless the Custodial Parent has a significantly higher monthly income than the Noncustodial Parent. The Income Share Method can also help Noncustodial Parents when both the parents' incomes are high, depending on the state's method of calculating child support. Many believe that the income shares model is fairer to the Noncustodial Parent. It is, at a minimum, a move in the right direction especially in correcting situations where the Custodial Parent is very well off and the Noncustodial Parent is struggling to make ends meet.

"The Melson Formula is a more complicated version of the Income Shares Model, which incorporates several public policy judgments designed to insure that *each* parent's basic needs are met in addition to the children's."[12]

PERCENTAGE OF INCOME METHOD

A *significant minority* of states use the Percentage of Income model to calculate basic child support obligations. These states set basic child support obligations *entirely on the Noncustodial Parent's monthly income*. But even in these states, Child Medical and Child Daycare Costs are often prorated according to the parents' combined total income.

The National Conference of State Legislatures has a website listing which income method, either the "shared income" or the "percentage of income," is used in each state. It's called the Child Support Guideline Models by State.[13]

---

12 Child Support Guideline Models by State, *www.ncsl.org › Issues & Research › Human Services*
13 www.ncsl.org › Issues & Research › Human Services

BEFORE-TAX INCOME VS. AFTER-TAX INCOME

The states are also divided on whether they use before-tax income or after-tax income to calculate the Noncustodial Parent's child support obligation.

The states that only request gross taxable income instead of after-tax incomes have adjusted their calculations to account for the likely taxes paid by obligors. Both types of approaches have their positive and negative sides in estimating an obligor's actual disposable income for child support purposes.

The procedure used by the "after tax income" states to determine the obligor's "net income" is obtained by deducting *all federal and state income taxes* along with any other *mandatory* payroll withholding like Social Security, Medicare, union dues, dependent health insurance, and "mandatory" retirement contributions from an obligor's income. Note that "voluntary" retirement contributions are generally *not deductible* to reduce gross income.

The states which use *before-tax income* reason that this method helps prevent Noncustodial Parents from shielding their true income through tax loopholes and tax deductions.

CHILD SUPPORT UNDER JOINT PHYSICAL CUSTODY

When a judge orders joint physical custody to be shared between both parents, the rules for calculating child support change dramatically. There are two variables used in the calculation of child support. The first variable is the percentage of "parenting time" allotted by the judge to each parent. The second variable is the relative income of each parent compared to the couple's combined income.

Recall that the judge orders parenting time based on some fraction (e.g., fifty-fifty). This is the first variable used to determine if, and how much one Joint Custodial Parent may owe the other in child support. The second variable used is each parent's income in relation to the parents' combined income. For instance, if the judge orders a fifty-fifty split in parenting time and one parent earns more income, the higher income parent will owe the lower income parent child support.

Court-ordered visitation time should not be confused with parenting time. *Visitation time does not reduce the Noncustodial Parent's support obligations.*

As mentioned earlier, the so-called exception to this general rule is the "extraordinary visitation credit" which several states have adopted. In Iowa for instance, the extraordinary visitation credit only applies if there are over 127 *court-ordered, scheduled overnight visits* with the Noncustodial Parent. The extraordinary visitation days are credited similar to the same way parenting time is credited when there is a joint custody arrangement.

ARREARS

An arrears (a.k.a. arrearage) is *the term used to define the total amount of past-due child support that an obligor owes.*

True, some obligors intentionally skip out on support payments because they think the system is unjust or loathe paying their hard-earned money to their ex. There are also many Noncustodial Parents who respond to Custodial Parents who illegally deny them visitation rights by withholding them child support payments. Universally, the denial of visitation rights is no defense for nonpayment of child support.

The law makes it clear that support obligations are not contingent on the Custodial Parent's denial of parental visitation rights even though every state says it's illegal to deny visitation rights to Noncustodial Parents.

Contrary to public opinion, there are many child support obligors out there who simply are unable to keep up with child support obligation through no fault of their own. People lose jobs, have health problems, suffer financial losses in their own businesses, and can face other countless financial difficulties. The economy goes up and down. There is also an epidemic problem for hardworking, lower-income obligors who are simply unable to make ends meet due to an unreasonable Support Order that has not been tailored for the obligor's ability to pay.

The burden of having to motion the court for "Changed Circumstances" is 100 percent on the back of Noncustodial Parents should these types of situations make it impossible to meet child support obligations. Procrastination, procedural rules limiting the frequency of these motions, and inability to pay attorney's fees can compound the situation.

Our culture and the court system have little sympathy for payers with financial difficulties. Regardless of whether or not some obligors simply don't have the financial means to make timely support payments, they are often labeled "deadbeat dads," scorned by society, and punished by the courts.

Child Support Officers and judges are often callous to obligors who claim they simply can't make ends meet. They hear it every day. As you will note in the next chapter, there are a host of punishments and sanctions dished out to those who get behind in making support payments.

There is somewhat of a silver lining to this dark cloud for those who owe child support arrears to the state (as opposed to the Custodial Parent). When a Custodial Parent draws welfare on behalf of herself and the children, the Noncustodial Parent owes the state for those welfare benefits received by the Custodial Parent. Under various state laws, all or part of that portion of those arrears can be forgiven under certain preconditions.

"In an effort to reduce or potentially eliminate uncollectible debt, some states use debt compromise, a process whereby a state settles a portion or all of the child support debt owed to the state by a noncustodial parent. Child support enforcement agencies in 29 states operate fully implemented or pilot debt compromise programs, and another 17 settle arrearage debt on a case-by-case basis. Of the 29 state that have debt compromise programs, 24 are fully implemented and five are pilot programs. The remaining five states do not allow compromise of arrearages."[14]

In an addition to forgiveness of child support arrears owed to the state, some state child support agencies (i.e. state Human Service

---

14 *www.ncsl.org › Issues & Research › Human Services*

agencies) can also stop mandatory interest from accruing on child support arrears. Both the debt of past child support arrears owed to the state (but not to the Custodial Parent) and on the interest being charged on the remaining arrears, have preconditions. The precondition usually is that the Noncustodial Parent has been making payments on current obligations for a set period of time (e.g. two years). The national Conference of State Legislators has excellent website showing each states policies in regard to forgiveness of arrears along with citations to each respective state laws.[15]

DEPENDENT CHILD TAX EXEMPTION

Under the federal tax code, the Custodial Parent is automatically entitled to the Dependent Tax Exemption. *However, a judge can order that the Noncustodial parent is entitled to the Dependent Tax Exemption!* If you are going to end up being the Noncustodial Parent paying Child Support to the Custodial Parent, I'll give you a good tip: have your attorney petition or motion that you are entitled to the Dependent Child Tax Deduction.

The *Dependent Child Tax Exemption* provides a significant reduction in federal and state income taxes. On top of that, the parent with the Child Dependent Tax Exemption *also currently* receives a direct dollar-for-dollar tax decrease in personal income taxes with the *Child Tax Credit*. The Child Tax Credit was worth one thousand dollars for the 2012 tax year, and was extended for five more years under the Fiscal Cliff Bill.[16] Any good tax accountant should be aware of any deductions, credits, or exemptions that you could be entitled.

How does the judge transfer the child Dependent Tax Exemption from the Custodial Parent to the Noncustodial Parent? Increasingly, judges are willing to *order* the Custodial Parent to sign and fill out IRS Tax Form 8332 which transfers the Custodial Parent's automatic right to the Dependent Tax Exemption. But conditions are usually attached to the orders which transfer dependent exemptions to the Noncustodial Parents.

---

15 *www.ncsl.org › Issues & Research › Human Services*
16 Details of Senate bill averting 'fiscal cliff by *The Associated Press | Associated Press* – Tuesday, Jan 1, 2013

The condition usually requires that the Noncustodial Parent must be "current" on support obligations at the end of the tax year. Conditional orders requiring transfer of the Child Dependent Exemption for the prior tax year can be confusing if not written properly.

Did the judge mean that the obligor has to be "totally current" at the end of the year, *which means no arrears, period*? Or did the judge mean that the obligor had to be simply *current on the total child support owed for the year, including the mandatory extra amount each state requires obligors to pay in addition to reduce their arrears (about 20% extra) when the obligors are behind on their child support?*

When a Noncustodial Parent asks the judge for the Dependent Exemption for income tax purposes, it's a very reasonable claim. After all, it's the Noncustodial Parent who has to pay taxes on the income used to pay for the child support payments, not the Custodial Parent.

If it is in your cards that you're going to be the Noncustodial Parent who has to pay child support to the Custodial Parent, have your attorney petition or motion the court to allow you to be the person who receives the Child Dependent Exemption. In the judge's mind, it helps prevent child support not being timely paid, which in turn means less work for the judge down the road in Contempt of Court motions for late support payments.

Asking for the Dependent Exemption is an excellent strategy for Noncustodial Parents. If successful, you can save many thousands of dollars on income taxes over the years. You have everything to gain and nothing to lose. It is also an excellent bargaining chip that can be used in settlement negotiations with your opponent.

INCOME TAXES

Basic Child Support payments cannot be claimed as a tax deduction by the Noncustodial Parent making the payments. Likewise, basic child support *is not* considered income for the parent receiving the payments.

Child Medical Costs *are* an itemized tax deduction for the parent or parents actually making these payments.

The amount of Child Daycare Costs paid by Noncustodial Parents is tax deductible. The Child Care Credit is only available to Custodial Parents even if the Noncustodial Parent pays for Child Daycare Costs.

As mentioned in the prior subsection, the tax code automatically gives the Custodial Parent the tax exemptions for their children *unless* the judge to orders that the Noncustodial Parent is entitled to the exemption. The parent who has the Dependent Child Exemption will also receive the Child Tax Credit. The Child Tax Credit terminates the year the child is seventeen years old. Prorating the tax year when the child turns seventeen is not allowed on the Child Tax Credit. But prorating is allowed on the child tax Exemption for the year the child reaches the age of majority.

Joint Custodial Parents usually share these tax deductions and credits according to the percentage of parenting time. Determining who should receive the exemptions for the minor children can be a fertile topic when negotiating settlements or motioning for a deviation from the child support guidelines.

MOTIONS FOR CHANGED CIRCUMSTANCES

Either party can request a "motion hearing" to either increase or decrease the Noncustodial Parent's support obligations due to Changed Circumstances. A motion hearing for Changed Circumstances is usually a short formal hearing where a party requests the judge to rule in their favor on an issue. The opposing party can "counter-motion" at the hearing on the same issue raised or raise a new similar issue.

Some motion hearings by necessity take a longer time to afford each side adequate Due Process than others. The Court Rules of Civil Procedure apply to motion hearings, including evidentiary rules and notices to the opposing side.

An argument supporting a claim for Changed Circumstances basically states that at least one of the factors used to calculate child support obligations has significantly changed since the judge last ruled on the support order. A significant increase or decrease in the Noncustodial Parent's income is the most common ground to request a change in the child support obligation. Another ground to motion for changed circumstances is that child daycare costs are no longer necessary because the child has grown older.

Universally, court procedural rules limit motion requests for Changed Circumstances. There must be a *significant change in circumstances.* They also limit the frequency of motions requesting changes in child support obligations. For instance, the increase or decrease in the Noncustodial Parent income or support obligation, as calculated by the child support guidelines, has to be over a certain percent—which is usually about 20 percent. The procedural rules also require a minimum time lapse has occurred since the judge last ruled on the issue—say for example, three years.

NO RETROACTIVE CHANGES IN PAST CHILD SUPPORT OBLIGATIONS

As a general rule, *prior* court ordered child support obligations can only be forwardly changed. This prevents any changes to past child support obligations even if warranted, except of course in cases of actual fraud.

However, *if no child support has been previously ordered,* judges often retroactively establish an order to an earlier date when the couple either separated or began the divorce proceedings.

When child support obligations are ordered, it's common that statutes have clauses in them that will automatically increase child support obligations yearly to account for increases in the cost of living.

CHAPTER 15

CONTEMPT OF COURT AND ENFORCEMENT OF COURT ORDERS

Judges demand respect in their courtrooms. They also expect that their court orders are to be followed—or else. The consequences for failing to submit to a judge's authority can result in the judge finding the offender to be found in contempt of court.

A person can be immediately found in contempt by acting rude or disrespectful to the judge in the courtroom. But the most common way of being found in contempt of court is to violate a prior court order. The vast majority of contempt of court actions in family law court are the result of failing to make timely child support payments. The main weapon in a judge's enforcement arsenal to sanction a person found in contempt of court is to order the person to be jailed.

Besides having the power to order an offender off to jail, judges have other weapons in their arsenal to enforce prior court orders. These weapons include, but aren't limited to, ordering wage garnishments, garnishing unemployment benefits, social security garnishments, federal and state tax refund interceptions, bonus interceptions, suspension of driving privileges, suspension of professional licenses, probation, fines, along with other similar and sometimes even creative forms of coercion and punishment.

Every state has its own laws to go after parents who are late in making child support payments. The most common avenue is in civil court using civil contempt of court motions. For those intentionally avoiding child support payments, the states and the federal government have all enacted criminal laws to use against offenders. They all authorize judges to use rather nasty forms of punishment and coercion to force obligors to make timely support payments or suffer the consequences.

MOTIONS FOR CONTEMPT OF COURT

Motions for contempt of court are surprisingly common in family court. Most contempt motions are filed when a party fails to make timely child support or alimony payments. Motions for contempt of court also arise from violations of restraining orders, which order a person not to do something, like hide or destroy marital assets. Violations of major restraining orders like "no contact orders" or "protection orders" are criminal law offenses.

Contempt of court motions are usually filed by the party benefiting from a prior court order. Under certain circumstances, child support officers will step in and file a motion on behalf of payees for past-due child support obligations. Child Support officers will step in if the payee is on welfare or if the payee requests their services after a payer is several months behind on payments (the trigger is usually about three months past due). When child support officers are involved, the district attorneys (who prosecute crimes) may represent the case, even though contempt of court actions are usually civil court cases.

Judges find other forms of behavior contemptible. For instance, never destroy marital assets, seize control or hide marital property, change the locks on the family home, or engage in any other type of behavior that could be considered improper or harassing. These types of actions are not only contemptuous, many are also criminal. You will do irreparable harm to your family law case if you find yourself in a barred hotel wearing complementary orange pajamas for a contempt of court violation.

CIVIL CONTEMPT VS. CRIMINAL CONTEMPT

There are two different types of contempt of court hearings. The most common contempt hearings are called *civil contempt of court hearings*. The second more serious types are called *criminal contempt of court hearings*.

The typical issue involved in civil contempt of court hearings is to determine whether someone violated a prior court order, and if so, what the appropriate court sanctions or remedies to force compliance of the prior court order are. There are limits on the length of time a judge can order an offender jailed for civil contempt under state law. The length of time for civil contempt usually cannot exceed ninety days.

The burden of proof needed to impose sanctions for civil contempt of court is a "mere preponderance of the evidence," which simply means "more likely than not" or "better than fifty-fifty odds" that an offender violated a prior court order or showed obvious disrespect toward a judge.

The legal theory behind bringing a civil contempt of court motion is to force the offender into compliance, not to punish the offender. There's an old saying often used to describe the enforcement of a civil contempt of court ruling: "when a judge orders an offender to jail for civil contempt of court, he sends him to jail along with the keys to his release." The "keys to his release" requires that the offender comply with the judge's order, like forking over late child support payments or disclosing the location of hidden marital assets. In the real world, the distinction between merely forcing compliance and actual punishment is a blurry distinction often amounting to intellectual dishonesty.

Criminal contempt of court is a criminal offense, as the name indicates. It's an extreme form of contempt that the judge feels undermines the court's power and authority. There are also state laws that make it a crime for violating certain court orders like restraining orders. Criminal contempt is prosecuted using criminal court procedures. The legal theory here is to punish the offender and set an example to others. In a criminal contempt of court case, the prosecution must prove "beyond a reasonable doubt" that the defendant had the intent to commit contempt of court and that the defendant's actions amounted to contempt of court.

USE COMMON SENSE

If you act disrespectful to your judge, you will be angering the person who is going to decide your fate in family court. If provoked enough, the judge may issue an immediate contempt of court order.

Don't place yourself in the position where you could be found in contempt of court. If you are found in contempt of court for whatever reason, I assure you that your judge will have a grudge against you. Don't put yourself in a position where the judge very well may rule harshly against you for the remainder of your divorce proceedings.

Judges do make wrong decisions and rulings. Even if an order against you is unjust or even just plain stupid, there's no good defense for violating a court order. If you're interested in pissing off a judge, a good way to do it is to inform a judge, either verbally or nonverbally, that a prior court ruling was unjust or that he or she is stupid.

I said earlier in the book that the uninformed often fall into avoidable pitfalls in family court. A contempt of court charge is one such huge, avoidable pitfall. You do not want the judge to have a bias against you or, worse, come out gunning for you for the rest of your divorce proceedings.

CRIMINAL DEADBEAT DAD LAWS

There are federal and state criminal laws used to enforce child support. They are commonly nicknamed "deadbeat dad" laws by women's advocates. The label itself is inflammatory and blatant discrimination. Violations of these laws can be felonies. A person found guilty of these laws may also find themselves on a public list of deadbeat dads used for personal and public scorn. County sheriff's departments sometimes use these lists.

Every state must follow the Federal Uniform Interstate Family Support Act to crack down on payers who move to another state to avoid having to make child support payments. This Act requires all the states to use their own legal system to enforce child support orders that originated in different states.

The Federal Deadbeat Punishment Act allows federal criminal prosecution for obligors who move to another state with the intent of skipping out on paying child support payments. There is growing international support for the creation of international laws to punish those who flee abroad to escape paying child support in their home country.

If it is in your cards that you find yourself being obligated to pay your opponent child support, and if the injustice of the whole matter makes you feel you should skip the state, or even the country, you better think again. Your state's Department of Human Services probably will find you, and you may end up facing criminal charges. Who says this country has outlawed debtors' prisons and involuntary servitude?

If you leave the country to escape paying child support, your United States passport will probably be revoked. Child support debtors at risk of skipping the country may find their passports revoked or denied prior to leaving the country.

One way they find "skippers" is though tracing social security numbers and driver's licenses. Any time someone applies for a job, banking services, renews a driver's license, buys a car, opens a bank account, rents something, opens a telephone account, gets pulled over for a traffic violation, or opens any utility account, the person doing so will likely be able to be traced using computer databases.

Shockingly, the federal and state legislatures along with judges' approval are in affect criminalizing past-due civil debt. Other civil debts, *except* those owed to the government for taxes and federally guaranteed student loans, can be discharged in bankruptcy court—not so with child support or alimony. No rock whatsoever is left unturned to squeeze out child support payments from noncustodial parents who become late in making child support payments.

A person who intentionally skips out on support payments and is found in contempt of court or found guilty of violating a deadbeat parent law out of pure spite is a fool. There is nothing to be gained by being spiteful, even if you have a legitimate complaint. You will find little sympathy from others regarding your real or perceived injustices if you are found in contempt of court for failing to make child support payments.

Support payments often create a tremendous burden on the noncustodial parents who have limited or insufficient finances to begin with. They receive little pity from the court system and society in general, due in no small part to women's advocates.

If you are a payer who is able to make ordered payments, do so, even if it creates an excessive burden on you financially. You will find little sympathy from child support officers and judges for financial hardship. That unfortunately is the nature of the beast. If you fail to make support payments for whatever reason, you will be making a bad situation worse.

If you are truly unable to make court-ordered payments, make sure the judge and the child support officer is made aware of the facts. Create a paper trail for evidence purposes. Have your attorney make a motion to reduce the payments so that you can explain your situation based on a change of circumstances. Never act or look like you are angry. Judges easily pick up on nonverbal communications, and they are also pretty good at lip reasing common cuss words. They don't like it. Hold back that hateful courtroom glare at the other party. Simply put, don't make a bad situation worse.

Unfortunately many people find themselves in contempt of court simply because they have been ordered inflated support payments beyond their financial capability to comply. Recall that the main factor to determine child support and other support orders is based on the payer's net income. A disturbing problem is that states are increasingly allowing judges to impute a payer's income to a level higher than a payer is actually making. This occurs regularly to the unemployed. These types of laws can lead to terrible injustices.

If you find yourself in a situation where you are simply unable to make support payments under the circumstances, get your paperwork together and have your attorney motion the court to modify your support order based on changed circumstances. Consider motioning the court for the child dependent tax exemption to reduce your income taxes for the children you are paying for. Cross your fingers and hope for the best.

FEDERAL CONSUMER CREDIT PROTECTION ACT

Federal law does shield payers of child support to some degree. Currently the federal Consumer Credit Protection Act limits child support garnishment of a payer's net income to 60 percent of a payer's disposable (after-tax) income and 50 percent of a payer's disposable income if he or she is supporting a new spouse and dependent children.[17]

The Consumer Credit Protection Act also shields child support obligors from many consumer debt creditors from wage garnishment. The Act states that wage garnishments from *other* regular debt creditors cannot attach if over 25 percent of the payer's net income is already being garnished. Family law support obligations take priority over any other creditors, including the IRS. Because child support garnishments often exceed 25 percent of a payer's after-tax income, wage garnishments by "other consumer" creditors cannot be enforced until the payer's child support obligations fall below the 25 percent limit.[18] If a payer's child support obligations are less than 25 percent of a payer's net income, the other consumer debt creditors can garnish the leftover amount *up to* the 25 percent maximum.

---

17 Title III, Consumer Credit Protection Act (CCPA) (15 USC §1671 et seq. (PDF) *(http://www.dol.gov/whd/regs/statutes/garn01.pdf)*; 29 CFR Part 870*(http://www. dol.gov/cgi-bin/leave-dol.asp?exiturl=http://s.dol.gov/8V&exitTitle=www.ecfr. gov&fedpage=yes))*

18 "Title III's restrictions on the amount of wages that can be garnished do not apply to certain bankruptcy court orders and debts due for federal and state taxes." United States Department of labor, Employment Law Guide-Wage Garnishment *www.dol.gov/compliance/guide/garnish.htm*

Debt creditors acting on behalf of the Department of Education are only allowed garnishment up to 15 percent of a payer's net income per month. In addition, federal student loan garnishments cannot increase a debtor's total garnishment *over* the 25 percent garnishment maximum limit under the federal Consumer Credit Protection Act. If a debtor is already being garnished over 25 percent or more for child support, the federally insured student loan debt collectors are prohibited from garnishing any wages until the debtor's total garnishment is under 25 percent of the debtor's after tax income.[19]

There is nothing pretty about sanctions and the techniques used to enforce court support orders. There are very legitimate constitutional questions regarding the means used to enforce family law support obligations. What you don't know about the law can hurt you. Ignorance of the law is no defense.

INEQUITIES IN THE LAW

It seems contradictory to common sense to punish obligors who are unable to keep up to date with child support by suspending their driver's licenses and professional business licenses. It's a not-so-subtle threat to the payer that if he doesn't pay up, the payer will lose all his or her income potential altogether, and risk becoming homeless or be at the mercy of family for support.

Many hardworking middle to lower income men who have been ordered to pay hefty child support obligations often find themselves in the financial twilight zone of having to live at, near, or below the poverty level. This can and often does lead to bitter resentments, especially when payers cannot make ends meet. Child support obligations are paid without any assurance whatsoever that the money will actually be used for the benefit the child.

---

19 U.S. Department of Labor Wage and Hour Division Fact Sheet #30: The Federal Wage Garnishment Law, Consumer Credit Protection Act's Title 3 (CCPA)

I recently read an eye-opening article on Wikipedia.[20] The following is a direct quote from that site: "According to a California study, 76 percent of the $14.4 billion in child support arrears in California has been attributed to 'obligors' who lack the ability to pay... In California, the "deadbeat" parents had a median annual income of $6349, arrears of $9447, ongoing support of $300 per month."

The US Department of Health and Human Services collects data from their affiliated state child support agencies. Recall that not all child support payments are collected through state child support agencies. Child support is often paid privately to the Custodial Parent from the Noncustodial Parent.

In the year 2010, data from the Federal Department of Human Services showed that the state Departments of Human Services collected $26.6 billion dollars in current child support payments from the $32 billion dollars that came due that year. Two thirds of that came from wage garnishments. At that time, there was $110 billion dollars in past-due child support arrears on the books from prior years. Over 11.3 million cases had past due child support arrears in 2010, reflecting a yearly increase each year over the prior five years.[21]

Bankruptcy is not an option to discharge unmanageable support obligations. Child support, alimony, state and federal taxes, and federally guaranteed student loans are all not dischargeable in bankruptcy court. It's not even "until death do you part." They'll go after your estate if you die before paying up.

If you were ordered to make child support payments directly to the custodial parent, make sure that you make payments with checks that are traceable unless you want to be at risk of having to pay for them twice to a thief.

---

20 en.wikipedia.org/wiki/Deadbeat_parent   Citing a report made for Califorinia Department of Child support Services, March 2003,

21 *FY2010 Preliminary Report | Office of Child Support Enforcement ...* *www.acf.hhs.gov › Office of Child Support Enforcement*

In conclusion, don't allow yourself to be subjected to the numerous punishments for failure to make support payments, or violate any other court order that orders you to do, or not to do something.

CHAPTER 16

THINK WHAT YOU WANT, JUST KEEP YOUR TRAP SHUT

It's plain old-fashioned common sense *not* to talk recklessly about personal matters, especially legal matters. Yet people often find themselves doing so to their detriment. Why? I just don't get it.

When you get a gut feeling that you shouldn't be talking about something, just don't talk about it! Don't get suckered into disclosing personal matters just to fill a void in a social conversation or in response to someone sticking their nose into your personal business. Any sensitive personal matter regarding your divorce should only be told to others on a need-to-know basis. This standard probably means you should probably just keep your trap shut regarding your divorce issues. If you obsess in public or private about what a jerk your opponent is, it raises issues on your own character, whether deserving or not.

When you talk about controversial personal matters, even to a trusted friend or family member, you're risking being blindsided later on by negative gossip. Gossip and rumors have a nasty way of becoming distorted each time they're passed from one person to another. The last thing you need during a divorce is to be the focus of negative gossip. Gossip and rumors also have a nasty tendency to find their way to those who may not be all that fond of you, including your opponent.

Don't feel that you have to explain the facts of your case in detail after being falsely accused of something or feel that you have to respond to half-truths or rumors to set the record straight. Simply deny the matter as being a falsehood. If a conversation is heading toward your personal matters, just say that you would rather not discuss the matter. Bad news travels fast, and the resulting rumors, whether true or false, can easily end up as your enemies' ammunition.

When someone rattles another person's cage, it is human nature to feel hurt and angry and lash back verbally. Angry people often find themselves saying things they later regret. Intoxicated people are particularly notorious for saying things they later regret because they either temporarily "lose their edge" or they are just plain foolhardy to begin with. I'm sure you've heard the old expression "loose lips sink ships."

In a criminal setting, police officers get suspects to say something incriminating by taking advantage of the suspects' ignorance along with the tendency of everyone to talk too much when under stress. A common police approach might sound something like this: "It's hard for me to believe that you're a criminal. I'd like to clear up this matter and be done with it. Will you help me clear up this matter?" Criminal suspects fall for the bait-and-trap game all the time, *even after* they have been given their Miranda warning.

The Miranda warning must be given to criminal suspects when they are in police custody before they are questioned. If the police fail to do so, any incriminating statements obtained cannot be used against them in court. *Police custody* means that the suspect is *officially* under arrest. The Miranda warning states that "anything you say can and will be used against you in a court of law." Translated, the Miranda warning simply means that defendants don't have to, and shouldn't, answer any police questioning when in custody.

Every time someone asks me advice on criminal matters, it reminds me of the day I applied for a public defender position. On a late Friday afternoon, I scurried over to the district's chief public defender's office just before the deadline for submitting resumes. I put my resume on top of a stack of about one hundred resumes. About a week later, I was interviewed by the chief. I found myself waiting in line with a handful of other fancy dressed wannabe public defenders. Statistically, I knew that I didn't have a chance of getting the job, and I wasn't about to kiss butt.

At the beginning of the interview, the chief gave me a hypothetical. She said, "OK, you are sitting at your desk in your office and your defendant client has just seated himself; what is the *first thing* that you do?"

I really didn't know the right answer, nor did I really give a darn given my expected chances of landing the job. I responded to the chief as if she were a defendant: "Just keep your damn trap shut about this matter! Don't talk about *anything* regarding this matter to *anyone* other than me, your attorney. Understand?" I felt a bit embarrassed because my answer could have easily been interpreted as being disrespectful, even though that wasn't my intent.

The chief smiled and later asked me, "Will you accept the position of assistant public defender?" Frankly, I was shocked. Unbeknownst to me at the time, I had just scored a bull's-eye. Later, after defending many criminal defendants, I fully realized why: an amazing percentage of defendants talk themselves into jail simply because they don't keep their trap shut.

The point I'm trying to make is simple. To their detriment, people talk too much because they often fail to recognize the possible consequences of blabbing too much.

Commit yourself to not disclosing personal, sensitive matters before the inevitable personal questions are asked. Do so even if you have nothing to hide. There is no reason why you should be caught off guard. If someone catches you off guard by asking you about a personal, sensitive matter, resist the natural temptation to respond directly to the question. It's usually best to say that you just don't want to talk about it.

If you are asked a question in a court proceeding by your opponent's attorney or asked directly by the judge, never ever volunteer information that is irrelevant to what you are being asked. Just answer the question without elaborating. The same principal applies to pretrial discovery requests.

DISCOVERY REQUESTS

One of the basic premises in civil court cases is to allow *open discovery*. If specifically requested, any facts relevant to the case must be disclosed by law to the other side. The theory behind open discovery is to allow either side to prepare fully for trial. Equally important, it allows each side to intelligently and ethically negotiate with the other side fully knowing that each other's cards are on the table. The attorney-client privilege is an exception to open discovery. There also exists the doctor-patient privilege, which can be overcome if a litigant raises his or her health as an issue in the case.

Discovery requests involve either the asking of formal questions relating to the relevant facts of the case or requests for documents relevant to the case.

If the questions are relevant to the case and not otherwise improper according to the court rules of civil procedure, litigants are required to comply with legitimate discovery requests. Failure to respond to a legitimate discovery requests is a ground for the other side to motion the court to *compel disclosure* or for a contempt of court motion. Judges have little tolerance for failures to comply with legitimate discovery requests.

Your attorney can object to discovery questioning if the objection is reasonable according to the rules of civil procedure. The judge has the final say to sustain or deny any objections to discovery requests.

The most common objection to a discovery request is that the information sought is totally irrelevant to any of the issues before the court or that the evidence is privileged due to doctor-patient privilege or attorney-client privilege.

For a relevancy objection to stand, the discovery requested must be totally irrelevant. Judges will allow questions that have even the slightest amount of relevancy, but will not allow questions that have absolutely no relevancy to the issues involved in the case, especially if those questions are harassing or inflammatory. Take, for instance, a discovery request asking a person if he is an atheist, an adulterer, or a communist. Chances are likely such a question is inflammatory and also totally irrelevant to the issues in the case.

Another objection to discovery is a request that creates unreasonable burden on the person asked. Take, for example, a request to see a copy of every single check a person has written for the last ten years along with all receipts, tax records, and phone records for the same period of time.

A person can also object to answering a question that could incriminate that person under the Fifth Amendment protection against self-incrimination. A question regarding a person's involvement in tax evasion or pushing drugs would fall into this category.

TYPES OF DISCOVERY REQUESTS

There are several types of discovery requests. An *interrogatory* is simply a formal written list of questions requesting written answers to the questions asked. After writing down the answers to the questions, the responder must sign an oath statement at the bottom stating that all the answers are truthful to the best of the responder's knowledge.

A *deposition* is a recorded verbal testimonial session outside of the courtroom. The parties must mutually agree upon the time and location of the deposition. The person being deposed is required to take an oath as to the truthfulness of the answers. Depositions are either recorded by an actual transcriber or video and audio recorded. Just like in an actual courtroom, the witness can be cross-examined at depositions. The two main differences between actual courtroom testimony and deposition testimony are that depositions do not occur in a courtroom and that judges are never present during depositions.

A *request for documents* is a request to hand over to the other side copies of documents that are relevant to the case. Requests for documents can include copies of tax returns, deeds, titles, mortgages, bank statements, and any other relevant materials.

Discovery and evidentiary rules are complex, and failure to provide relevant discovery information can be used by your opponent as grounds for a motion to compel discovery or, even, a contempt of court motion. It is important to have an attorney help you if the opposing side makes discovery requests. All discovery answers are given under oath as if given in an actual court proceeding. False answers to discovery requests can be criminally prosecuted as perjury or as grounds for contempt of court.

You can save your attorney time and save yourself money spent on attorney fees if you do most of the legwork for discovery requests. If you are requested to answer interrogatory questions, write down your answers to them in the order asked and submit them to your attorney in an organized manner for your attorney's review. If you are requested to provide relevant documents, once again, submit them to your attorney in an organized manner.

ABUSING DISCOVERY

Open discovery is a powerful tool to get to the facts of a case, especially regarding financial matters like income and asset possession. Your case may or may not include discovery requests. Discovery requests are fairly common in family court, so don't be surprised or intimidated if discovery is aimed at you. But discovery is sometimes overused and abused as a strategy to overwhelm and intimidate an opponent. This type of bullying tactic has a way of backfiring and finding its way back to its source with retaliatory discovery requests. For attorneys, excessive discovery requests to and from an opponent aren't necessarily bad news—it's easy money in billable hours to the client.

Use common sense regarding discovery requests served on your opponent. Chances are you know what information, if any, you need from your opponent. Keep a leash on your own attorney. Excessive boilermaker interrogatory requests may be inappropriate in your case. Excessive discovery costs each side needless attorney fees and frustration.

Discovery is an important tool in family law litigation—but use it wisely. There may be facts and documents in your opponent's possession that you may need for your representation. Make sure that you obtain the entire discovery you need, and resist the temptation to intimidate your opponent with excessive discovery. Courts award attorney fees for needless litigation expenses, including frivolous discovery tactics.

If your opponent is using excessive discovery or doing anything else as a tactic to harass and drive up your attorney fees or needlessly intimidating you, talk to your attorney to see if motioning for attorney fees would be appropriate. Requests for attorney fees are not that uncommon during nasty divorces. Judges can and do award attorney fees to the other side as compensation and punishment for causing needless litigation expenses and delays.

COURT OF PUBLIC OPINION

The "court of public opinion" is not a legal court at all. It is a social court where all the people who know you or who have heard about you are the judges of your character. There is no reason to put your character and reputation at issue by voluntarily entering yourself into the court of public opinion with family, friends, or acquaintances. Don't feed the inevitable rumors.

Idle talk can easily make you a defendant in the court of public opinion. The following old and admittedly crude expression explains this matter very succinctly: "the more that you stir the shit, the worse it stinks."

DON'T FUEL THE FIRE

Avoid intimidating your opponent or assassinating her character. However tempting it may be, don't scorn your opponent with foul or demoralizing language in or out of court. Such language angers judges regardless of the truthfulness of the statements being made. Using four-letter words or belittling comments will do *nothing* to further your cause. It will only infuriate your opponent and end up hurting your chances for a successful resolution of your divorce.

Remember that one of your main goals in family court should be to come up with a settlement agreement that is fair and reasonable to both sides. If you allow yourself to get into a pissing match with your opponent, you can forget about any fair settlement agreement.

You and your opponent are more than likely bitter and resentful to one degree or another. What was true in William Shakespeare's day is also true today. He once wrote, "Hell hath no fury like a woman scorned." Choose your battles. Do not get into a fight you cannot win simply out of spite. Our society not so subtly seeks to protect the so-called weaker of the sexes. That concept has a strong foothold in family court, and it's the very foundation of the discrimination men face today in family law court.

The only person you should talk to about matters that are relevant to your family law issues is your attorney. Hiding a bad card from your attorney doesn't make it go away. To properly represent you, your attorney should know all your family court cards—all of them.

CHAPTER 17

RESTRAINING ORDERS, AN OFTEN ABUSED BUT NECESSARY EVIL

Restraining orders are court orders which order a person not to do something. In the family court setting, the most serious type of restraining order mandates that an offender have no contact whatsoever with a victim for the victim's protection. These types of restraining orders are called *protection orders*. Some jurisdictions refer to them as *orders for protection*. Protection orders are designed to prevent future aggressive behavior. To obtain one against an aggressor, a victim must sign a sworn statement describing at least one incident of criminal abuse by an aggressor. Protection orders are often simply called *restraining orders*. They are quite common in the family law environment.

Protection orders are an effective deterrent against domestic abusers to protect their victims from future violence. The downside is that they are given out like candy to children on Halloween to those who cry wolf. This can and does lead to abuses by those seeking an unethical advantage over their opponent to resolve their family law issues. There's even a mind-set that if a woman gets into a heated argument with her husband, a restraining order is appropriate. "After all, everyone else does it. I just don't want to have to deal with him anymore."

Besides our society's general ignorance of the legal grounds for obtaining protection orders, there's an element of self-righteous vindictiveness. It's a powerful weapon in the hands of those wishing to have the last say in an argument. It's also a powerful weapon to gain a strategic advantage in family court and demoralize an opponent.

The current abuse by women who fraudulently obtain protection orders against their husbands during their divorce is epidemic and unconscionable. The tactical gains to be won in divorce court are huge while the punishment against this type of behavior is all but nonexistent.

The problem is compounded because there is an incredible lack of due process for a fair and impartial hearing on the merits of the allegations used to trigger the legal use of protection orders. Many wrongfully accused often do not contest abuse allegations due to the fact that an allegation of abuse creates a rebuttable presumption that the victims' allegations are true. When a man gets into a 'he said, she said' situation at a protection order hearing: Who do you think is going to get the benefit of the doubt?

There is also an incredible lack of due process at protection order hearings which grant temporary alimony, child custody, and child support for the alleged victims who request them. Temporary child custody rights transferred at a protection order hearing blow away the other side's position regarding permanent custody in the final divorce decree. It's a travesty of injustice for those wrongly accused.

Nonetheless, the immediate relief that women can get by slapping a restraining order on their husbands *is a very necessary, but often abused evil.* Often, 'time is of the essence' to prevent violence, even if it means striping away an alleged abuser's Constitutional Due Process rights to a fair and impartial hearing.

What needs to be changed in our court system is to *actively punish* those who fraudulently file for protection orders. That simply isn't being done in our court system today. The threat of being charged with perjury isn't a real threat at all because of the magnitude of the problem and the current lack of enforcement for abuses of the system.

Most people don't even realize that the minimum statutory threshold to obtain this type of restraining order requires *at a minimum*, at least one minor criminal act of aggression like a push or an implied threat of an assault. Even threatening to hit or slap someone without doing it by waiving a fist is an example of a low-level criminal assault if a reasonable person would believe it was a treat. Many states specifically classify *criminal* harassment and criminal stalking as grounds for protection orders as well. Criminal harassment requires *at a minimum* that a defendant intentionally caused severe emotional distress on the victim and that it would cause emotional distress on any reasonable person as well. However, the crime of criminal harassment in most jurisdictions *also requires* a reasonable believe that the victims feared for their safety.

Swearing, insulting, or merely expressing anger without a real or implied threat of physical harm or offensive contact does not meet the minimum grounds for obtaining a protection order. Alone, these types of unbecoming behaviors do not rise to the level of being an assault or a threat of an assault. Like it or not, arguing and cussing at someone are forms of protected speech under the First Amendment's right to freedom of speech.

So, how does a person obtain a protection order? A person claiming to be a victim can simply visit the local county courthouse and ask for a protection order application. They come on preprinted forms where the victim fills in the blanks. The victim must write down a sworn statement stating that he or she is afraid of an aggressor, explaining why the alleged victim needs a protection order against an alleged aggressor.

A judge will make a decision based entirely on the victim's written application. At this stage of the protection order process, no input is allowed from the alleged aggressor. In fact, the alleged aggressor is not even informed of this informal ex parte process. *Ex parte* simply means that only one side is allowed to give any evidence. The alleged victim's written application for a protection order is assumed to be truthful, and cannot be contested at this stage of the legal process.

The judge simply reads what the applicant wrote about the aggressor's conduct which lead the victim to be afraid of the aggressor. If the judge determines that there are sufficient grounds in the application as defined by the state's statutes specifying the grounds for obtaining protection orders, the judge signs the protection order. A statement saying "I am afraid of him because he might hurt me the way he acts" is probably a good enough reason at this stage for the judge to find a ground to slap a protection order against someone.

After the protection order is signed by the judge, it's hastily delivered to the county sheriff's office. A sheriff's officer then immediately hunts down the alleged aggressor and serves the protection order. After service of the protection order, the alleged aggressor is bound by the no-contact order.

Protection orders *often* (but not always) include a summons to appear in court on a later date. It depends on state law and whether temporary legal rights are requested by the victim in addition to the no-contact order. If a protection order hearing is scheduled, there will be a summons to appear on the matter possibly in as little as ten days after a protection order was served. If the alleged victim is seeking temporary possession of the home, alimony, temporary child custody, and child support in addition to a protection order, a summons to appear in court will be ordered. At the hearing, the issue of whether the judge should grant the victim's request for extra temporary rights from the aggressor will be addressed. When receiving a summons to appear in court on such a short notice, respondents/defendants are often ill prepared to deal with all these matters, not to mention finding good legal representation.

If summoned on a short notice, strongly consider requesting a "continuance" to have the hearing rescheduled for a later date. This can be done through the Court Administration office (if that is possible), or upon a motion to the judge at the hearing to allow you time to be prepared to address the court on these issues at a later date.

If a hearing on the matter is not automatically scheduled because the victim didn't request extra temporary rights, the alleged aggressor can request a hearing to rebut the allegations. The hearing can give an alleged aggressor an opportunity to challenge the allegations if the alleged aggressor chooses to do so and can provide evidence that the alleged victim was lying.

Because protection order hearings are civil court matters, the preponderance of the evidence standard (i.e. more likely than not) is used. This low standard of proof actually favors the alleged victim because the initial presumption is that the alleged victim is more likely than not telling the truth (rather than beyond a reasonable doubt).

What many don't realize is that automatically scheduled protection order hearings are mainly used to determine temporary monetary benefits for the alleged victim along with granting the alleged victim temporary sole child custody rights. If an alleged aggressor chooses not to contest the protection order, the issue becomes what temporary rights and monetary benefits can the alleged victim get from the alleged aggressor.

Alleged aggressor's due process rights to a fair hearing vary from jurisdiction to jurisdiction and must be thoroughly researched before arriving at a protection order hearing. Whether the victim requests temporary benefits like alimony, child custody, and child support often depends on whether the alleged victim checks those boxes on the protection order application form.

If you should happen to be served with a protection order, read and understand everything in the order, including the scheduling date and what the alleged victim is asking for. If there is not a hearing scheduled, you should be given notice on how to schedule a hearing to contest the matter. Have an attorney represent you who actually practices criminal law cases!

Protection order hearings are civil court proceedings based on allegations of criminal wrongdoing against a victim. Because allegations of criminal wrongdoing are necessary to trigger a protection order, the allegations can also lead to criminal prosecution if the District Attorney feels the evidence is sufficient to warrant a criminal case.

Once a protection order has been served, a violation of the protection order is considered a serious crime, even if the protection order was obtained fraudulently. Never ever violate a protection order. Consent by an alleged victim to get back together with an accused aggressor is not a defense! This is true even if the person benefiting from a protection order doesn't want to press charges for an aggressor's violation of a protection order. This can even include a situation where a couple peacefully walks down a street together hand in hand! If one of them has a protection order against the other and a police officer is aware of that fact, the person with the protection order against him or her will get arrested even over the protest of the person who petitioned for the order. It's black and white. Yes, this actually happens; in fact I've seen it happen during my practice.

The legal reasoning behind why full due process is lacking at protection order hearings regarding temporary legal relief (like child custody and alimony) is that an alleged aggressor can receive adequate due process in later court proceedings. The problem is that a bias against the accused forms in the minds of the important players involved in a family law case—including the judge!—for the remainder of the divorce proceedings. It can be a game changer on family law issues.

Another problem with granting an alleged victim additional relief along with a protection order is that temporary benefits—including child custody, child support, possession of the marital home, and alimony—can become permanent rights simply because of the reluctance of judges to change the status quo regarding women's rights. This is particularly true regarding child custody issues. A protection order early in the proceedings usually cuts off a husband's chance for custody, even for joint child custody. Remember that old saying "possession is nine-tenths of the law." Besides that, judges show little sympathy toward perceived abusers and come down hard on them during the course of the divorce proceedings.

Domestic abuse is like any other type of evil. Evil has no gender preferences. Human character traits of good and evil are spread out equally between the sexes. Our family law court system just doesn't seem to understand that simple fact, or care about it. Doing evil is really only a matter of choice regulated by the opportunity to inflict harm, and a person's morals or lack of thereof.

Victims of domestic abuse include not only women, but also men, the elderly, and children. Sure, all too often men are the ones committing domestic abuse, but the vast majority of men going through a divorce are not domestic abusers.

If you are slapped with a protection order based on false allegations, you should fight it if you have *evidence* to prove the allegations are false, or if the allegations against you do not meet the statutory grounds for the judge to grant a protection order. For instance, if one spouse simply tells another off in an argument without threatening the person, that person is protected under the First Amendment right to free speech. When an alleged victim is outwardly lying in an application for a protection order, the alleged aggressor's only recourse is to catch the liar's lie, if possible.

Based on a true story, following is an ad-libbed example of protection order misuse. For purposes of the example, let's call the alleged abuser Joe, and the alleged victim Angel Face. After an argument, an Angel left the family house for her mother and stepfather's place in protest. At a minimum, she was mad and wanted to embarrass her husband. She had been in an ugly mood for several months now from just prior to after the birth of the couple's child.

The next day, Angel decided to go ballistic and up the ante by getting a "restraining order" to kick Joe out of his premarital home. Researching on how to get a restraining order, she found out that she could go to the court administration office and fill out an application. Angle found out there was a little problem with her plan. She found out from the application that she had to write down under oath why Joe's behavior that gave her a reasonable belief she might be in physical danger. She wasn't going to let that stop her, so cooked up a web of lies as her reason.

She stated in her application for a protection order that she had to leave for her and her baby's protection the prior day and hide out at her parents place. She stated that she saw Joe stalking her by driving by repeatedly in his brother's new car.

She stated she returned to her home today about an hour ago and found the whole house "trashed including the baby's room!!!" She said she left immediately to file a protection order because she feared for her and her baby's life.

With the ink on the protection order still wet, an irritated police officer tracked down the Joe at work. In front of others including a client, the officer loudly read the alleged abuser's statements of Joe's alleged abuse and gave him notice of that a protection order hearing was scheduled in 14 days. Along with broadcasting Joe's alleged bad acts, the officer notified him that the Protection Order stated that his wife was also seeking temporary alimony, child custody, child support, and possession of his premarital home. He then stated, "If you fail to appear at the scheduled Protection Order Hearing, a bench warrant will *issued for your arrest!*" After repeating that he will be arrested and jailed if he neared his home, the officer stated that he would escort him to his house Joe wanted to "pick up a few clothes and toiletries."

Joe was totally freaked out, but at least he had enough common sense to take the officer's offer to go out to his house and pick up a few clothes and toiletries. Joe had a plan. He went to *every* room in the house to look for clothes with the irritated police officer tagging a few feet behind. Joe then addressed the officer, "I was accused of trashing the whole house, and my wife said she fled in fear just a short while ago. You've been in every room in this house, your trained officer, have you noticed any evidence that this house was trashed?"

The officer's demeanor changed. "No, I haven't. At worst, I noticed was the house could use a little tidying. There's no evidence that this place was trashed recently as she stated."

Before the scheduled hearing, Joe called his father-in-law. He stated he was at his home the night before when the alleged incident occured and knew nothing about Angel's allegation that was Joe stalking her at his home.

Joe subpoenaed the police officer who witnessed Joe's house wasn't trashed to testify at the hearing. He also subpoenaed the step-father who knew nothing of the allege stalking at his house. Joe also requested his brother and his wife to testify that Joe had never had even been in their new car, and therefore it was impossible that Joe was stalking Angel with their new car. Joe also requested two other couples who were friends of both the Joe and Angel as character witnesses against Angel.

In this example, the Angel left a tangled web of lies which could have, and should have been disproven with witness testimony. In this instance, Joe would have been a fool not to expose Angel's vicious plot to get the upper hand just prior to her filing for divorce.

I have represented clients in both family law and criminal law. I consider filing a false protection order petition against a spouse a criminal act every bit as vicious as armed robbery and every bit as emotionally devastating as rape. Under our present family court system, there are absolutely no effective safeguards against this rampant abuse other than relying on an individual woman's morality.

I represented two different women who obtained protection orders while in the process of divorcing their husbands. Both divorce cases required protection orders against their husbands due to aggravated assaults with deadly weapons. With both cases, death threats were involved along with loaded firearms pointed at the victims. As their attorney, I did indeed support my clients getting immediate protection orders. I even considered getting a protection order for myself after hearing a rumor involving a death threat against me involving one of these cases.

Don't get me wrong, quick and easy accesses to protection orders are also appropriate in far less dangerous situations involving domestic violence. No one should feel threatened, even with a threat of low-level assault, which by definition is also an assault.

On the other hand, I've seen people abusing the system. In one case a woman wanted me to represent her in a divorce. She also wanted to obtain an immediate restraining order on her husband in order to "kick him out of the house." Because of her demeanor, I was suspicious of her. I told her that I would have to find out more about her situation before I agreed to represent her.

I asked her if he had ever abused her. She responded, "Yes, all the time. He doesn't do his fair share to keep the place clean. He argues with me. He has the nerve to have his friends over on the weekends. They shout at the TV when watching sports while drinking beer and smoking cigarettes!"

Then I asked her, "Has he done worse things to you? For instance, has he hit you, slapped you, or acted in a way that made you think he might physically harm you?"

Her answer was always no. Eventually I had to tell her she didn't have the legal grounds to slap a protection order on her husband. She kept insisting that I take a large retainer fee. "Just make it happen with the restraining order and kick him out of the house!" I didn't know if she was just ignorant or trying to bribe me. She obviously didn't know that all she would have had to do was to go down to the courthouse and fill out a protection order application.

I finally said, "Look lady, what you are asking me to do is unethical and illegal. I am not interested in representing you because you are asking me to help you obtain a bogus protection order. You're wasting my time." I hung up the phone in protest.

Being slapped with a protection order is largely avoidable. If your marriage is on the rocks or if you are already in the process of a divorce, resist the temptation to blow your mouth off. If you are wrongly accused and have evidence to fight it, get an attorney and fight it.

If you crossed the line and there are legal grounds for a protection order against you, keep your damn trap shut, get an attorney, and try to let the matter blow away. Probably the best alternative is to plead "no contest" where you don't have to admit anything either way, rather than having all the dirt being exposed to the judge at the hearing with live testimony. Everyone makes dumb mistakes, especially in emotionally charged situations. Try to regroup and deal with it. Look forward and focus your attention on actually being a nice guy who happens to be in a divorce.

CHAPTER 18

HOW WOMEN CAN ABUSE
THE LEGAL SYSTEM

Divorce often brings out the worst in people. There's money to be had, egos to defend, and scores to settle. The darker side of human nature and feelings of anger, jealousy, greed, and a sense of entitlement can turn people into ruthless adversaries.

Ruthlessness and other character flaws are equally distributed between the genders. There are quite a few people who have few qualms about wrongfully predating on another's weaknesses if given the chance. The current unfair advantage that women have in the family court system provides women opportunities to exploit the system, and exploit the system they often do. Anger and greed often become key motivators on both sides to exploit for personal gain and to inflict emotional pain to settle a score or feed one's ego.

I am in no way suggesting that women are more sinister and conniving than men. Most of us are well aware of how devious and hateful men can be toward their spouses. What I am saying is that the law and the enforcement of the law are so far out of whack in protecting women's rights that it makes it too easy for women to exploit the legal system.

Given the darker side of human nature, the current court system actually *encourages* exploitation by women because punishment for this type of behavior is all but nonexistent, while the gains are quite high for those who wish to predate on their former partner. The main type of predatory behavior I am referring to is lying under oath. The Bible calls this type of behavior "bearing false witness." I call it "fraud on the court."

Even when the blatant perjury of a woman is exposed in family court, it is usually swept under the rug as being merely the hysterical ranting of an emotional woman who exaggerated the truth. "The poor thing, she is just going through a period of emotional upheaval. There must be a good reason why she is so traumatized and upset. Things will be OK, dear."

Think defensively. You've been given clear notice in the last chapter of how women often obtain bogus protection orders against their husbands come divorce time. If you *don't* have a restraining order against you and your former honey wants to talk, it's OK to talk. I advise *not* meeting in private, especially where she is living. If you must meet, consider meeting in a public place, like at a restaurant, but only if you think it might be to your benefit in negotiating your family law issues. But be careful. Expect phone calls to be secretly recorded. Don't allow yourself to be set up. Also remember my motto: think what you want, but just keep your trap shut.

If a protection order has been served on you at your wife's request, stay away from her and have no communications with her whatsoever unless you want to spend some time in jail. Don't allow your emotions to delude you; she doesn't want to talk to you. All settlement negotiations must be done through your attorney to her attorney once a restraining order is in place.

This is a final word of caution: If you have children and have been given visitation rights, keep in mind that it gives women ample opportunity to do mischief and harm. It is common that children become either intentionally or unintentionally indoctrinated against the noncustodial parent.

Remember that the secret for women seeking to abuse the legal system for their benefit is to lie and exaggerate the truth so as to make them look victimized, whether physically, psychologically, emotionally, or economically. Often, it includes all the above. The more a woman can portray herself as a victim, the better her chances are for financial gain and vindictive retaliation.

Keep your own head on straight. When emotionally charged, it is easy overreact to lies and exaggerations alleged against you. How much of a defense should you put up? It depends on what is at issue and the relative importance and relevancy to your family law issues. I'm not saying don't expose lies and exaggerations against you. What I am saying is to think before you react; and when you react, do so strategically. Keep in mind that all the strategic decisions you make should be based on reason, not on emotions or ego.

Remember the old saying "the more you stir the crap, the worse it stinks." This certainly applies to many, if not most, situations when mud has been slung at you in family court. Often it is simply best to deny things that have been falsely alleged against you.

CONCLUSION

Face it, going through a nasty divorce is like being forced to play a high-stakes poker game with the cards stacked against you. Each side was dealt an original set of cards at the breakup. You're going to have to work a little harder to even the odds. New cards are dealt. The outcome of the game depends partly on the initial cards that have been dealt, the new cards that might be dealt, and partly on how each side plays its cards during this gut-wrenching game.

If your cards on a particular issue are poor, don't up the ante and waste your cards and credibility on a losing hand. Keep your eyes open for new cards and opportunities to level the playing field. Your starting point for developing effective strategies is to put your reasonable-guy hat on and think before you act. One of the best cards you could be dealt is to have a reasonable opponent. You might even come out of this ordeal far better than expected. Yes, it does happen more than one would think.

One of the most important strategies you should have when going through a divorce is to try to avoid a nasty divorce and come up with a negotiated settlement with the opposing side. A settlement agreement should be as fair as possible to each side. If an issue is important and your odds are good, don't be afraid to play your litigation card against an unreasonable adversary. Let your adversary lose credibility on a losing hand, not you. Always play your cards wisely in the family court environment and be prepared in advance. Develop effective strategies based on your family law street smarts and follow them. Be dumb like a fox and don't act out of spite.

For better or worse, you will survive this ordeal. Don't allow your divorce to destroy you. Remember that you will have good times in the future, but only if you make it happen.

It's important to remember we all have to be survivors and try to enjoy our brief existence on this planet. You can do your share of good on this earth and make it a little better place for everyone. Start with making it a better place for you to live.

For now, be a survivor and better your odds by planning your moves strategically. You've learned the tools to do just that. You've been shown the fundamental principles of the law and how judges use that law to resolve family law issues. You've gained insight into what to expect from the other players involved in your case and how to deal with them strategically in the family law environment.

Play your cards the best you can with minimal regret and resentment. Tomorrow is another day. Soon you will be able leave this chapter in your life in the past and move on.